Poetics of the Creative Process

An Organic Practicum to Playwriting

Femi Euba

UNIVERSITY PRESS OF AMERICA,® INC.
Lanham • Boulder • New York • Toronto • Oxford

PN
1661
.E933
2005

Copyright © 2005 by
University Press of America,® Inc.
4501 Forbes Boulevard
Suite 200
Lanham, Maryland 20706
UPA Acquisitions Department (301) 459-3366

PO Box 317
Oxford
OX2 9RU, UK

All rights reserved
Printed in the United States of America
British Library Cataloging in Publication Information Available

Library of Congress Control Number: 2004113585
ISBN 0-7618-3004-9 (clothbound : alk. ppr.)
ISBN 0-7618-3005-7 (paperback : alk. ppr.)

∞™ The paper used in this publication meets the minimum
requirements of American National Standard for Information
Sciences—Permanence of Paper for Printed Library Materials,
ANSI Z39.48—1992

To my dear wife, Addie, comrade-artist
broaching the *illud tempus* of the creative process.

Contents

Introduction		1
	Drama and the Playwright: *From Concept to Structure*	
1	The Creative Potential: *The Tragic and Comedic Quest to the Illud Tempus*	14
2	Mythic Expressions of the Creative Process: *The Fateful/Fatal Paradox*	31
3	Ritual Impulses and the Playwright: *The Dramatic Structure*	52
4	Visible Dramatic Vehicle and Its Ritual Implications: *The Central Character*	74
5	Ritual Scope: *The Monologue and the Creative Challenge*	88
6	Ritual Scope and Developments: *The One-Act and the Full-Length*	104
Conclusion		
	Ritual Efficacies: *The Ilud Tempus Script*	129
Appendix I		
	Organic Practicum: *Development Exercises*	131
Appendix II		
	A One-Act Monologue	141
Appendix III		
	Ritual Registers: *Analysis of Text*	149
Bibliography		157
Index		161

Introduction

Drama and the Playwright:
From Concept to Structure

The attempt to give a definition to the creative process, with a view to finding an organic approach to playwriting, has led us back to the cornucopian offerings and intimations of ritual, for possible answers. For a creative process is after all a ritual process. This analogy, as extensively argued in my book, *Archetypes, Imprecators and Victims of Fate*,[1] identifies the dramatic structure of a ritual process, consisting of a "need," the "sacrifice(s)" that the need demands, and the "efficacy" of the sacrifice or sacrifices, an achievement which may or may not be successful—that is, in terms of what is desired. In drama such elements easily compare with an objective (of the central character), the conflict created by obstacles to the objective (demanding the "sacrifice" of the character), and the consequence realized by the sacrificial persistence of the character to the objective—which ultimately may or may not be what the character desired..

As such, ritual, along with its components, easily fits into any discussion of drama and, consequently, into processes of drama, which begin with the playwright. In this book, I not only seek to show the connection between the ritual process and the creative process of the playwright but also to externalize the seemingly abstract process, the stages of which begins in the playwright's psyche with the generation of an idea, which subsequently becomes concretized on the blank page as action and dialogue, ready for interpretive performance by actors and literary interpretation by audience and critics. To be able to explicate this process in practical terms can only advance rather than limit the writing stage, in a way that is not forced but demonstrable as an organic approach to playwriting. Hence, the present effort to write a playwriting text, among many on the market, is not so much how to write a play as how the play evolves in the creative process and therefore its implications.

The implications, however, ultimately address the components of a play and the act of writing.

Several years back, a graduate student in creative writing at Louisiana State University where I teach, asked me, "Why is playwriting so marginalized in this (English) department?" Specifically, she was referring to the way it seemed to have been given less focus in the graduate handbook. My immediate reaction was, "But it isn't?" But she continued to insist, "It is, it is! Not just in this department, but in general."

Rereading the handbook later, I realized what she was talking about. But I failed at the time to see what she implied as a general fact, especially given the numerous textbooks on playwriting, and the many workshops now available to playwrights. Thinking further, especially about the recognition first given the playwright as the poet or artist of the theater in the classical period, I could argue that there has been a downshift, or displacement, of that recognition, which renders the playwright's creative integrity and status somewhat commonplace. While I will not go into the history of that displacement, I will mention some possible contributing factors.

The first seems obvious. Television and film have endangered and continued to hamper the legitimate power of the theater. Along with that abrogation of power, perhaps in an indirect way, an attitude of mistrust has developed toward the drama text as an evocative accomplishment of one individual. Often a screen script is the work of many scriptwriters; so, what is seen on the screen is a far cry from the idea and expression of the original creative author, even if that author still bears the sole rights. The collaboration, of course, may be for a good cause in terms of the development of the script, but the fact that the production is a shared expression often erodes the author's creative authority. In the theater, this process of erosion would seem to have begun with the emergence of the director, and had magnified with television and film.

It must be emphasized that a collaborative effort, or revision assistance, in constructing a workable script or production is not new to the theater. In fact, it is the nature of theater that plays are workshopped and productions are a collaborative effort of set, costume, and lighting designers under the vision of the director. However, a point that may be argued is that playwrights in the past, especially in the classical period of Greece that Aristotle wrote about, and in the time of Shakespeare, playwrights as well as being originators were a crucial part of the production collaboration and revision. Also, overall, a playwright benefits from the vision of others, which often extends the playwright's vision in a positive direction, helping the playwright see what he or she probably intended but may not have realized. But what the television and, especially, film seem to have done to collaborative effort, by incremental revision of the script, is to negate or devalue the individual source of idea and expression, resulting in less focus on the creativity of the person who manifested the idea and expression, and more on the commercial initiative that the collaboration fostered.

Another contributing factor to the marginalization of the playwright is the way the public has come to regard drama in isolation of its author. For instance, various attempts have been made to express a workable definition of drama, all to the exclusion of the person who has made drama possible. A recent TNT commercial, obviously geared to promoting its various drama programs, and of course to impact the awareness of its viewers, sought the thoughts of some notable personalities in show business. Each came to the conclusion that drama is about life (in terms of conflict, love, anger, hate, death, etc.). Some attempted a concrete metaphor for an otherwise abstract definition of drama, such as, "Drama is a rubber band that could snap," or "Drama is life at a hundred sixty-nine miles per hour." In short, the commercial contended, drama is all what life is supposed to be but somewhat intensified by its form and compactness.

Although the commercial presentation gave a fair assessment of drama overall, it based its definitions more on the final product, the performance, than on how the drama came into being. The work and art of the playwright was a foregone conclusion, or relegated to the background as insignificant.

On second thoughts, the viewpoint of the commercial and its, perhaps unintended, oversight of the playwright is conceivable and appropriate—it was meant for viewers, most of whom see only the finished product. But for the curious observer, this viewpoint raises pertinent questions: What is the process of the drama? How does such drama come into being? What has the creator to do with the finished product? Even if the finished product excludes or marginalizes its originator, does the originator have no creative claims to the success of the spectacle? Or, in the case of an unsuccessful production, does the originator share the blame? While I do not attempt to answer such questions directly in this book, I do hope to reinstate the playwright's creative experience as the primal force in theatrical endeavors, charting the creative experience from the generated idea in the creative psyche, to the expression of that idea on paper or computer. I hope not only to ascribe merit where it is due, but redefine the attitude toward drama with the playwright in mind.

A third contributing factor to the marginalization of the playwright makes the endeavor of writing this book more worthwhile. As if in agreement with the sensational and commercial aspirations of television and film, most books on playwriting have dealt on how to write a play, the elements of drama to be considered, and the writing skills needed. On the whole, the books focus on the technique of structure rather than the idea that creates that structure (what I have constantly referred to in this book as the idea-note that strikes the psyche), and the nature of the idea's inspiration and development. While these books probably offer essential information for the developing playwright, that information often tends to border on the formulaic. Furthermore, to be overly conscious of technique may impede the spontaneous flow of creativity, which presupposes the technique. Since the spontaneity is an impulse of an action whose idea pleads to be expressed, it seems imperative to understand the nature of that spontaneity in the psyche, and its relationship to the subsequent expression, after which technique appropriately can be applied.

At first glance, a focus on the inspirational may appear particularly abstract and therefore unproductive. But if it is possible to come to terms with some tangible image of this inspirational, the knowledge could be very beneficial to enhancing the structural. In other words, if it is possible to evoke or establish a visual perception of the dauntingly mysterious process of the psyche, combining this perception with the technique of the physical process, the first leading into the other, would present a holistic, organic approach to playwrights and their art. That is the intention of this book, to try to define the initial, inner gestational stage of the creative process, then use this construct to elaborate on the external writing stage, thereby increasing the vision or the level of awareness of the playwright and, I hope, making his or her expression more productive. Consequently, the book is divided into two parts, each defined in ritual terms. The first part deals with the psychical ordering of the creative process, in which a dramatic idea is conceived, or strikes like a note in music; the second part deals with the structural expression of that idea. But the parts are related, bound by similar ritual impulses of need, sacrifice and efficacy, and reflective of each other. Given this relatedness, the concepts expressed in the chapters often appear to repeat themselves. However, each repetition intends to develop a slightly modified perception of a particular concept, like a musical variation on a theme, with the view to giving the reader a fuller understanding.

While the ritual impulses of the creative process, from the psychic abstract to the visual concrete, unequivocally identifies drama as a ritual expression, a notion that argues well for playwriting as a source of dramatic expression, the impulses, it must be stated, are grounded in other performative arts, such as music and dance and, to a certain extent, the visual arts. As such, it is not unusual to note the association between these art forms and drama. On the other hand, musical works, dances, and paintings are often described as dramatic. And drama, in its representational or presentational form, variously puts other art forms to effective and emphatic use. Although the use of the other art forms may not be obvious to the playwright at the time he or she is creating the drama, it becomes inevitable in the interpretation of the drama on stage.

Hence, there is a symbiotic creative relationship between drama and other art forms, especially the performative. That relationship will be investigated in this book, however briefly, to see how this may contribute to the creative process, and help the playwright better achieve his or her objectives. For instance, the relationship between music and drama may yield some insights to the functioning of the creative process.

The incorporation of other performative arts in drama not only suggests that drama, especially as expressed in theater, is the most expressive of the arts, it also makes the creative challenges of the playwright more surmountable. David Cole, in *The Theatrical Event*, acknowledges the primal distinction of theater arts, whose performance alone combines *the present* of the physical events, which the other arts also express, with *the presence* of the dramatized imagined events evoked in words and action by the actor.[2] In other words, theater alone allows us to experience the irreconcilable fusion of the imaginative truth of performance with the present truth of the physical events. However, by making the distinction, Cole establishes certain concepts primarily for the actor, which the present book both challenges and explores for the playwright.

Rather than make a distinction between the creative expression of playwriting and that of the other art forms, in this the book I seek parallels with similar orderings of creative processes. Indeed, an understanding of music, perhaps the most abstract and cerebral, yet the most evocative, of all the performative arts, should place the form at the heart of the ritual impulses of the creative process, and therefore of playwriting. To appreciate the evocative nature of music, we only need to identify the prevalence of its impact in human experience. For music provokes so many emotions and actions—it makes us sing, dance, love, shed tears of sorrow or joy, be terror stricken, daydream, and so forth. When Shakespeare in *Twelfth Night*, through Orsino, says, "If music be the food of love, play on, /Give me excess of it, that, surfeiting, /The appetite may sicken, and so die," he acquaints us with one of the most mysterious and profound emotions that music evokes in human experience, that of love.[3] It is an emotion that has also been the most ritualized (dramatized) subject in drama.

Wole Soyinka, in *Myth, Literature and the African World*, gives us an idea of the ritual power and significance of music, which evolves from the depths of myth,[4] which Northorp Frye explains as the narrative of ritual[5]. Soyinka explores the power of music, albeit too briefly, with the Yoruba cultural evocation of it in the abyss of tragic despair. In doing so, he compares and extends Nietzsche's perception of it in its more formal and structured form in the European tradition, a system, Soyinka implies, that virtually impedes our understanding[6]. Similarly perhaps, the European dramatic tradition (by its technical development and linear-time constraints) has impeded our understanding of the ritual relationship of theater. In case we are in doubt about this assessment, we only need to refer to the way theater scholars and practitioners such as Victor Turner, Richard Schectner, Peter Brook have sought for pure forms of drama and theater in ritual-oriented cultures, such as in Africa and India, where music is a significant component of ritual. And then we must wonder why we use music so much in theatrical performances and productions.

Yet, despite our common love of dance or song, we feel the ritual power of music differently—whether in church, where the church pipe-organ, that king of musical instruments, intones a ritual enactment of spirituality or where the gospel singer cries out his or her soul; or in secular locations where a musician improvises jazz on a trumpet or a saxophone, or a rock singer yells in ecstasy of pain and joy. Perhaps then we can say that music is an essential creative force induced to express our individuality, our spirituality, and that its varying impacts are all relevant to the ritual intimations of the creative process. The word itself suggests its significance as a source of inspiration—Muse-ic—suggesting, if I may be so bold, what ekes out from the Muse(s) to sustain the creative psyche. With this in mind, I attempt in this book to extend Soyinka's concept and explications of ritual in an effort to link the psychical expression of the creative process with the physical, and subsequently to use the construct to explore the form and structure of dramatic writing.

The questions ultimately arise: how does one concretize an abstraction of the mind as a ritual entity for the playwright, and how does this help the playwright become more evocative and inventive? First we must take the Romantic view that a creative artist is quester for truth in the infinite variety of creation.[7] The playwright, as a questing artist, therefore, can be regarded as a priest-ritualist-interpreter of the dramatic idea, or Muse-ical note, that strikes his or her creative psyche. In the creative process, psyche is a microcosmic metaphysical space which the individual quests and broaches relative questions about life and death, seeking explanations, really questions of spirituality, in the macrocosmic metaphysical universe. In this regard, the playwright's expression is the product of a ritual struggle to elicit insights about how life works (socially, politically, economically, and so forth), and the probable ways of coming to terms with it. The playwright's product is encoded with ritual impulses, the vibrating Muse-ical rhythms of the metaphysical space and world.

For the playwright to evoke his or her Muse-ic, respond to it, and interpret it effectively, he or she, like any other conscious artist, indeed like any other conscious individual, must constantly contemplate the physical elements around (humankind, animal, trees, landscape, buildings, sounds, etc.), elements that constitute that individual's Muse-ic and help define the individual's spirituality. By spirituality, I mean everything that makes up a person's individuality—fate, character, temperament, culture, religion, and so forth. In any artist's created expression, through the compulsive singularity .of his or her individuality (really through his or her combative will to express), the artist fine-tunes the practical dynamics of his or her interpretation of the idea-note that struck, an interpretation that implicates emotional, social, sociological, psychological make-up of the artist.

The difference in interpretation for the playwright is that his or her dramatic interpretation is particularly functional and impactive, because his or her present/presence art responds to, and conforms with the dynamics of life, which is at once ritual and dramatic. For instance, while the musical artist expresses pure emotion, the dramatic artist expresses, at once, the emotion and the visual transmitters of that emotion (character, dialogue, thought, scenery, etc.), as well as sound (music) itself. Furthermore, the playwright concretizes these elements into a visible dramatic structure, through the medium of word-symbols, on the computer screen or printed page. Through that medium, the playwright is the psychic interpreter of the idea-note that struck; the actor, with the help of the director, is the physical interpreter of the playwright's resources and medium. David Cole's *mythos* of the theatrical event, unfortunately, places the actor, "at once a role-possessed body and the embodied role," at the ritual center of interpretation.[8] By so doing, I believe he takes for granted a significant prerequisite—the art of playwright or the author of the expression that possesses the actor. But to do so is to forget the struggle that goes on, at the initial stage of rehearsals, between the script, representing the playwright, and the actor trying to understand and come to terms with the playwright's script. However, I recognize the point David Cole makes, given the fact that the practical art of the actor, through that of the director, is also creative and, because of its dramatic intentions, follows a physical ritual development. In fact, an understanding of the actor's physical/dramatic development can aid the playwright's understanding and development of his or her creative process.

Indeed, the relationship between the playwright and the director or the actor is one that has been misunderstood in the shifting developmental stages of the theater. From the Greek classical period through the Renaissance, the playwright also performed the functions of the director and the actor and therefore was rightly seen as the artist of the theater. In this regard, Aristotle did not have any problem convincing his peers about the all-important central position of the playwright as the poet of the theatrical space, which represented not only the world of humans but also that of divines. However that pivotal position of the playwright was gradually usurped, first by the actor-manager of the eighteenth and nineteenth centuries, and then by the modern director, who from the beginning of the twentieth century has gained prominence as artist-godhead of the theater. The director's prominence is not unjustified, considering the gradual segmentation of societal values that has occurred through various revolutions to our modern world, compared to the more culturally cohesive classical world, and considering the necessary division of labor in a modern theater production by its diverse and monumental responsibilities.[9] But this development has not only obscured the entitlements of the playwright, it has obfuscated the symbiotic relationship that should exist between the playwright and his or her creative siblings and institutional associates.

In spite of Cole's emphasis on performance, his concept offers useful insights. Significantly, his evocation of the Latin phrase, *illud tempus*, has led us to probe the dimensions of the playwright's creative process. Actually meaning "that time," *illud tempus* suggests a particular time of and a particular space in an old world. Given a metaphysical dimension in relation to ritual, that time and that world evoke the world of ancestors and divinity.[10] Furthermore, when we examine the relationship between the playwright and the director and actor, that relationship, given the ritual implications of drama, places the interpretive, ritual medium of the playwright (like that of Cole's shaman/priest) in the *illud tempus* or the metaphysical world of the gods. It is a ritual arena the playwright enters, with "sacrifices," in order to receive the dramatic impulses of his or her Muse-ic, which are subsequently scrawled or expressed in word-symbols for characters, and coded, so to speak, with the theatrical resources of a drama script, what Cole designates the *illud tempus* script.[11] In this regard, both the director and the actor are the expressive interpreters of the playwright's medium, and their presentation or representation serves the devotees, the participating audience, the community that seeks insights (suggestive, apparent, objectified, or opinionated) that can engage them, and define for them a compact vision of the nature of the world.

To put the ritual implications of the playwright's creative process in a clearer perspective, this book will use examples from established dramatic works, both classical and modern. Two contrasting examples will suffice for now. In my playwriting workshop, Sophocles' *Oedipus Rex* and Samuel Beckett's *Waiting for Godot* have never failed to elicit various responses from my students. These responses provoke a need to investigate the structural and dramatic depth of the two plays, in order to understand their respective vision and the creative process of each playwright. For instance, the initial reaction to *Oedipus Rex* suggests that "Fate" is its subject, that is, what the play is about—a response that later proves, through investigation, to be not quite correct. To start with, fate is a metaphysical entity that is not easily supported by argument in literary criticism, for it is hardly practical to use a metaphysical entity to dramatize what is supposed to be a human objective. In this regard, Robert W. Corrigan's observation that tragedy is based on human struggles, as opposed to divine struggles, makes dramatic sense[12]. However, fate obviously pervades the fabric of the drama, and as such, its significance must be located. In *Oedipus,* fate is the part of Sophocles' classical vision that counterpoints the drama's subject with cosmic depth, and whose creative resources exist in the *illud tempus*, the metaphysical space broached by the playwright through a ritual immersion and struggle. To understand this process better, it will be necessary to establish the ritual arena of the *illud tempus* in more concrete terms.

According to Soyinka, ritual is the "drama of the gods" in which a questing godhead or priest dares inimical forces, broaching the abyss of the unknown with sacrifices to obtain certain knowledge. It is a traumatic process, one that almost wrings the life out of the questing individual, who comes near and, indeed, overcomes disintegration[13]. The outcome of this hazardous quest, however, is informative and rewarding, in terms of the knowledge gained for self or community. Soyinka, drawing copiously from his Yoruba culture, suggests that the divinity Ogun (god of metallurgy; principle of creativity; patron of the arts) was the first quester and artist to experience this perilous, fateful/fatal, but creative journey. The experience (that is, the combative will and sacrificial suffering of the all-too-human quester summoned up to brave the hostile elements) because of its challenges and nobility is a tragic one, making the quester a tragic figure.

A parallel figure in Western theatrical experience is not hard to find, and Soyinka has made such parallels in both critical and dramatic writing. The Greek Dionysus compares well with Ogun as patron of the arts, and in terms of the intense expression of his ritual of disintegration and restoration through his Bacchae, an experience which institutionalized the tragic form and the tragic spirit in Western theater.[14] These two figures, Ogun and Dionysus, by the nature of their experiences suggest a model for the experience of the creative process. Through their magical art, power of possession, and patronage, they have manifested the creativity of drama and theater among their various devotees—playwright, director, actor, musician, visual artist, dancer, and so forth. What this book intends to do for the playwright (an Ogunian or Dionysian artist), in order to make that psychical experience palpable and easy to evoke, is to try and relive the experience within the physicality of the devotee/playwright's artistic expressions—that is, the established plays that have obviously demonstrated the experience. Concretizing the psychical experience represents the first stage of the creative process. The second stage, which again makes connections with established dramatic expressions, goes on to develop form and content, that is, through the technical skills of playwriting.

As stated, the plays I shall be using as illustrations to physicalize and develop the creative process dramatize the fateful/fatal paradox inherent in the ritual/creative process, in the artist's rigorous journey to give expression to the idea-note that strikes his or her psyche. They also show, through the quester/artist's progressive ritual immersion and struggle, the dire nature, the anguish and the subsequent elation of success of the playwright. This condition not only is reminiscent of the experience of the primal artists (Ogun and Dionysus), it also legitimizes the dramatic expressions as visionary intimations of the gods' votaries. My contention is that all playwrights, whether classical or contemporary, experience the process as Ogunian or Dionysian artists, and such a supposition could extend to all creative artists in general.

The term "elation of success" needs some explanation. It is an exhilaration of satisfaction often felt by creative artists at the end of the creative process, which, however, does not diminish the tragic nature of the process. In this regard, it is similar to the inner satisfaction of a tragic hero or heroine regardless of the tragic confrontation and of the destruction or death that he or she may face. In fact, death is of no consequence to the tragic experience, which more importantly expresses both the combative will and the vulnerable fragility of humankind's heroic stance, a combination of conviction and error in judgment. For the tragic experience has to do with the singular and hubristic choice the tragic hero or heroine makes, daring the status quo, as it were—a choice which really is the only alternative, and inevitable because of the limitations inherent in the hero or heroine's character. It is a choice of action the hero or heroine would obviously make again if he or she were to relive his or her life, a choice that transcends death and is therefore celebratory. Such elation is well displayed in characters such as Oedipus, Lear, Othello and, befittingly, in the religious figure of Christ. It is displayed also in playwright's experience because of the singular, hubristic approach he or she takes, an approach, although engaging, that does not necessarily influence anybody, therefore somewhat ambitiously hopeless.

Let us put the fateful/fatal paradox in perspective. As stated before, *Oedipus Rex* is not about fate (an rather abstract entity); rather, it is about Oedipus' egotistic drive (visible through Oedipus' action), which impels him in a singular search for truth to a certain tragic error in judgment and catastrophe. However, fate is implicated, not because Oedipus has fled from the preordained force, which really is outside the action of the drama, but because of his character, which is fateful, apropos his stature and combative will, yet fatal with regard to the dogged choices he innocently but blindly takes.

Waiting for Godot also implicates fate, in fact even more directly than *Oedipus* because it is about the consequences of taking certain action of fate, waiting—that is, Estragon and Vladimir's act of waiting in hope for an unknown entity. The waiting is a fateful action because of the vague rewards it promises if Godot appears, yet fatal because that presence, and therefore what they hope for, may not manifest. The despair provoked by the paradox of their waiting initiates their characteristic clownish actions, which are used to control, the best they could, the anguish caused by that despair. However, this is a play of ideas, as opposed to a play of action such that *Oedipus* describes. Beckett tries to express these ideas in series of fateful/fatal images, such as those described by the master-servant relationship of Pozzo and Lucky; images that are also implicit in the poetic language of the dialogue and speeches.

Both plays, as dramatic expressions of their authors, ultimately articulate the playwright's inner states at the moment of creation, and the choices they had to make in terms of subject, theme, action, and character. More importantly, the plays indicate the anguish the playwrights suffered, which all creative artists suffer, the emotional tension that affects playwrights and their characters—regardless of whether the play is action-based, or idea-based. I shall in due course explain those two emphases of drama (action and idea) as involuntary, emotional choices that do not necessarily affect the dramatic quality of a play's structure.

All plays invariably deal with a certain fate of the characters, whether the central focus of the play is a character or an object or an idea. But more important is the expression of the fateful/fatal complex, what defines the spine of the play and pervades the sphere (metaphysical or physical) of the drama, which in turn exposes the creative complex of the writer. This sphere of drama, along with its storehouse of creative possibilities (which possibilities become the script) is the *illud tempus*, the chthonic world or ritual arena of creativity this book aims to bring to the awareness of the playwright (emerging or established alike) and, by extension, all creative artists. Such awareness may help the playwright understand his or her creative vision more clearly. However, the explication of creative process must be understood only as a guide. Just as technique must be used not to impede creativity but to enhance possible revisions, the concept of playwriting outlined in this book is designed to enable the playwright engage and participate in the creative process, not dominate that process.

The second part of the book addresses developing the visible construct of the creative process, the play's structure, as part of a total process. I have taken an organic approach, which has proved successful in graduate and undergraduate workshops I have taught over the years. In these workshops, the commitment to physical expression evolves gradually, first by understanding the creative process using the established dramatic expressions as illustration, from which understanding an idea strikes each student and, to everybody's surprise, a play is underway.

Since the visual is an important factor of drama, class exercises are initially focused on concretizing the abstract idea-entity, especially through emotive abstractions such as love and hate. Such words begin to take a life of their own in various contrasting images and implications. For within an imaged or visual construct lies dramatic potential, that is, the hidden impulses of structure, conflict and objective of expression. The subject of the play becomes visible from the idea that strikes through what is imaged, this subject materializes into a theme which suggests an action that raises consequences with that subject. For example, "Love" as a subject for Shakespeare's *Romeo and Juliet* is implicated by a consequential action suggested in its theme: "Love, a vial of sacred potion held by two young people, may be so contaminated by the curses of family feud that, when drunk, it becomes a reckless poison that destroys innocent lives." Such a drama-ready theme could easily evolve from the visual constructs or images that students have explored with the idea of love, the key that strikes a note in the psyche. However, as often happens, the situation for a play may be the first to evolve from an image or directly from the idea-note that strikes — for instance, the exploration of the image may take a concrete narrative of two virgin teenagers, boy and girl, whose fondness for each other is frustrated by familial, class or cultural differences. It is such dramatic impulses of theme or situation, through image, that will go on to negotiate characters, action and dialogue.

In pursuing the fateful/fatal paradox of the creative process in action, I have explored in this book an important exercise from my playwriting workshop — that is, the potential of the dramatic monologue. As is often the case in my workshop, there is an initial objection to a one-act monologue because of its seeming limitations in terms of character, conflict, focus, etc. But confronted with these limitations, the student becomes afflicted with a creative tension, a ritual struggle that provokes him or her to invent and create. The book explores an organic approach that should make it possible for the student to resolve his or her creative tension, as well as the limitations of a one-act monologue. More than this, because all the problems of character, conflict, action and focus become resolved, the monologue serves as an initial exercise that allows the playwright master the mechanics that should help develop a more regular one-act, or a full length play. Again, as stated, the explication of these concepts will necessarily overlap and often repetitively revised. In addition, three appendices have been provided at the end of this book. The first summarizes exercises that develop the writing of a monologue and regular plays; the second gives an example of one-act monologue written by one of my students; the third provides a summary of structural analysis of some of the plays discussed.

The scope of this book is by no means limited to the student, or the budding playwright. Using its approach, a practicing playwright may be able to resolve the creative problems that hitherto have eluded resolution. However, playwriting like all creative endeavor is 99 percent effort and 1 percent inspiration. One could interpret this to mean that the 1 percent inspiration is the generated idea, and the 99 percent effort is the ritual struggle exerted to express that idea, that is, with all creative resources at the playwright's disposal—for the dramatic resources of playwriting are difficult to grasp, evolve and resolve. Furthermore, dramatic content (with all its psychological or sociological dimensions) invented and ritualized is very much dependent on level of experience, exposure, awareness and cultural make-up of the artist/ritualist. But the struggle to achieve need not be in a vacuum, and the inspiration or the Muse-ic need not elude; there is a practical way of evoking it, which is the objective of this book.

NOTES

1. Femi Euba, *Archetypes, Imprecators and Victims of Fate: Origins and Developments of Satire in Black Drama* (Westport, CT: Greenwood Press, 1989).

2. David Cole, *The Theatrical Event*: A *Mythos, A Vocabulary, A Perspective* (Middletown, CT, Wesleyan University Press, 1975), 5–7

3. William Shakespeare, *Twelfth Night*, ed. George L. Kittredge, 2nd edition (Waltham, Ma.: Blaisdell Publishing Co., 1966), 1.

4. Wole Soyinka, "The Fourth Stage" in *Myth Literature and the African World*(Cambridge, England: University of Cambridge Press, 1976).

5. Northope Frye, *Anatomy of Criticism: Four Essays* (New Jersey: Princeton University Press, 1957), 105–109, 117–20.

6. Soyinka, "The Fourth Stage," *Myth,* 145–148.

7. For a concise description of the Romantic ideal, see Oscar Brockett, *History of Theatre*, 4th edition (Boston: Allyn and Bacon, 1982), 424–426.

8. David Cole, *Theatrical Event*, 5, 12–21.

9. For a concise development of this, see Toby Cole and Helen Krich Chinoy, eds., *Directors on Directing*: *A Source Book of the Modern Theatre*, revised edition (New York: The Bobbs-Merrill Co., Inc., 1963), 3–77.

10. For Cole's idea of it, see *Theatrical Event*, 7–11

11. Cole, *Theatrical Event*, 10. The concept is a slight departure from the one I offered in *Archetypes, Imprecators and Victims of Fate* which, like Cole's book, is based on performance. See *Archetypes*, "Introduction," 6–7.

12. Robert W. Corrigan, *The Theatre in Search of a Fix* (New York: Dell Publishing, 1973), 11–13.

13. *Myth*, "The Fourth Stage."

14. See Soyinka, *The Bacchae of Euripides*: *A Communion Rite* (W.W. Norton, 1974).

Chapter One

The Creative Potential: *The Tragic and Comedic Quest to the* Illud Tempus

The interpretation of the *illud tempus* script that David Cole assigns to the actor takes for granted a significant factor—the authorial creative process, that of the playwright, whose creativity is primal, and more rightfully takes us to the ritual arena in the metaphysical heartland, the psyche of the playwright. As such the playwright, as a quester to the arena, is the priest/interpreter of the dramatic impulses or messages constituting the idea that strikes his psyche or that has struck him. The playwright alone, in the absence of collaborating agents, is the primal priest/quester for a community of audience, known or unknown. On account of his or her receptivity to the needs of the community, or the needs the playwright has felt, the dramatic impulses are concretized in decipherable word-codes and images that constitute a script. It is this script, the efficacious product of the playwright's interpretation of the *illud tempus*—coded with music, action, scenery, and so forth, and informative with messages to the community/audience—it is this manifestation of the playwright's sacrificial immersion that a group of actors must attempt to interpret, through the unification-concept of the director.

But the actors' interpretation can only be an attempt, since neither the director nor the actor has the individual experience of the playwright. Both the director and the actors are trying, as best they can, to serve the community that the playwright presumes. In fact they are at the mercy of the community, which will react truthfully to the interpretation, whether it is a viable representation or not. Regarding the director and actors' attempted interpretation, a frequently favored procedure is evident—a director usually prefers a script that captures his or her imagination or sensibilities.

The actor then is a physical interpreter of the *illud tempus* script, as opposed to the playwright, the physical interpreter of the *illud tempus* dramatic idea. Furthermore the actor's art is more collaborative, in terms of not only the director, but also in terms of other actors, as well as scenic, lighting, costume designers, all of whose assistantship is almost inevitable. Their assistantship is necessary to the actor's interpretation of the script. In this regard, the actor's interpretation is limited, since, at best, the actor is copiously helped by the director's concept, within which the actor must try to contain his or her interpretation, even when, as sometimes happens, the actor is also the author of the script. But that interpretation comes to the actor, through some understanding of the character that the playwright has suggested, especially the central character, whom the playwright has used, principally to convey his or her coded messages. For the central character is the figure from the *illud tempus* who represents not only the voice for the archetypal messages but also, virtually, the community the character offers to serve. Technically, the character expresses one of the impulses of the idea, usually the most important, that strikes the playwright's psyche, impulses constituting the *illud tempus* script. The playwright must ultimately decipher and interpret correctly this central figure and the impulse he or she is trying to give expression to.

Many entities constitute the *illud tempus*. There is the ritual arena that evokes the idea-note that strikes; there is the idea itself, coded with sounds and images, messages that need to be interpreted; there is the expressed product of the playwright's sacrificial questing, the script. In terms of Cole's *mythos*, based on Mircea Eliade's shaman/hungan religious ethos, the coded messages act on behalf of the powers that be, whom the doubly heightened "priest," both the divine and community agency, approaches for answers to a particular crisis.[1] In terms of playwriting, the process can be described as follows: The playwright, compelled by some crisis in his world, racks his or her psyche for answers. Through this probing, an idea loaded with possible answers to the problem strikes, answers that the playwright tries to decipher, and struggles to interpret in a dramatic form. Thus begins the ritual expression that identifies the creative process of the playwright. As we shall see, the tragic and/or comedic impulses that develop with the idea-note that strikes depend on the playwright's bent and individual view of the world.

The felt experience of the ritual expression, to reiterate the fact, is relative to other forms of creative art, but it informs playwriting particularly because the form into which a playwright places the coded messages for his or her theater community is both ritual and dramatic—ritual in terms of the struggle to interpret, and dramatic in terms of the crucial consequential factors raised by the struggle, immediate and realistic experiences which both the playwright and his or her central character share. I shall come back to this. But consequently, unlike other creative arts, the art of playwriting registers at once the physical "present" and the imaginative "presence" in the theatrical space, which parallels the ritual arena of the *illud tempus*.

Regarding these parallel structures, we must acknowledge another fact—that everything abstract has its relative concrete construct, like a spirit or soul and the body. Traditional cultures such as in Africa or Asia understand this, hence their constant search in the metaphysical world for physical identities and their explanations of the metaphysical with physical realities in their mythologies—which often see god and human in similar retributive binds. Furthermore, acting has shown that an abstract entity such as emotion can be evoked physically in terms of action and reaction, or a memory recall, therefore the attempt to recreate an emotion as realistically as possible on the physical stage.

There is really nothing extraordinary about the need to give physical form to an abstract entity, or manifest the spirit in body, since it is the basis of all human development. It is an ever present human need to understand the unknown in palpable terms, and to give expression to an intoxicating poetic vision of an idea. Science has done much to demystify the magic of nature, much to the chagrin of lovers of mysteries and nature's phenomena. For mythmakers and believers in phenomenal occurrences, the demystification has raised a vital question, whether science has gone too far in its mechanistic probity and technological transformations. On the one hand, scientific facts contribute to the advancement of the world; on the other hand, they indicate possible danger, cause a loss of innocence, and constitute a loss of mystical resources and presences from which to create.

Actually, it is virtually impossible to impede the scientific and technological progress, which, not unlike mythmaking, probes the unknown and crystallizes the specific knowledge gained from that experience. The danger of science seems to lie not in the questing itself but in the application of the knowledge gained or the technology developed as a result of that knowledge. Misuse of knowledge is often at the cost of essence, the natural process of what is known and converted, whose essen-tial endowment to our understanding is often deliberately ignored, or discarded. Such an attitude describes the goal-oriented preoccupation and the mystical void of our modern society.

The deliberation of the two previous paragraphs, much as it may have sounded like a sermon, seeks to validate the initial stage of the creative process. For the playwright, as well as for other creative artists, the reflection validates the engagement of the artist's psyche by the crisis affecting his or her world, through which a creative idea-note strikes in the ritual arena of the *illud tempus*. The idea is coded with dramatic messages that are in need of interpretation. To interpret the messages, the playwright experiences the rigors of a ritual immersion through which the playwright expresses the codes in ritual/dramatic form. Depending on the constitution of the idea and of its vehicle, the playwright, the dramatic potential of the expression may be tragic or comic, or both. As such, the individuality of central character that manifests, to physicalize the idea, may be compelled by (to use a modern concern) a technological pursuit that has tragic implications, or the character might assume mechanistic traits that are comedic or satiric—such as ritualized in, say, Elmer Rice's *The Adding Machine*, or Richard Adler and Jerry Ross' *The Pajama Game*. However in the contemporary world, it is very difficult to emote purely in tragic or comic modes, because ideas, by the nature of our complex existence, are often coded with both.

But further to the void of mystical imagination created by modern progress, the attenuation of the power of ritual becomes a critical case in point. Like the gradual devaluation of the mystical "man in the moon," by the space-craft Apollo explorations, the magical and evocative value of ritual would seem to have been downgraded to notions of mere repetitive patterns, as some usages of "ritual" often suggest. Fortunately, serious creative artists have, consciously or unconsciously, always longed for the power of ritual, the muse-ic of the creative process, in an effort to grasp the nature of essence. Western artists have attempted to rediscover the lost experience by observing its performative forms in traditional cultures of Africa and Asia, where ritual still has significant presence. While the loss, the search and the rediscovery of ritual process have produced works of profound impact, such as Peter Brook's experimental and collaborative *Mahabarata*, Western artists' interpretations have often been hampered by the technical, and therefore abstract, system of codes that they have chosen to communicate the experience. Various examples of these, suffused in linguistics-influenced jargons of critical inquiry, are easily located in many abstract, expressionistic art forms in fine art, dance, language and even theater, such as the group rituals of the Liquid Theater and the Open Theater in the 1970's.[2] In fact, these developments can be described as products of our technological and mechanistic society.

My intentions at this stage should be obvious—to firmly establish the ritual identity and dramatic significance of the playwright's creative process that first begins with the idea-note that strikes his or her psyche. The question that logically follows is this: How does this idea strike, and what is the nature of it? While clues to this question will continue to develop in the following chapters, let us begin by acknowledging its particularity.

When Wole Soyinka, in his attempt to define music as a significant component of ritual, observes differences between African and Western forms, he not only correctly identifies these differences in the evocation of the experience, he strikes at the heart of the relationship of music to a dramatic idea. Like the other abstract components of ritual, such as time, language and natural phenomenon, music in its Western form has become so formalized that, although its power is often felt, that power has not been clearly understood, until perhaps recently when medical doctors began to investigate alternative therapies for terminal illnesses, such as cancer, and found music to be a therapeutic and restorative medium, similar to the power of prayer. The implied relationship of music and prayer is no accident; in both, an individual is able to confront his or her spirituality.

As Soyinka indicates, music is an evocative and invocative power-source of ritual. He exemplifies this with a chant that not only accompanies but invokes a ritual process, a dirge like chant that wells from the depths of despair and reaches into the metaphysical abyss to make connections with the self separated from the original oneness.[3] In the Yoruba world view, an individual consists of two selves, which were one before birth. At birth, the physical self, choosing his or her fate, separates from his or her metaphysical counterpart to live that chosen fate in the physical world. However, to be able to live the fate as chosen (since existence in the living world has obliterated any notion of that fate) the physical self must constantly invoke his or her metaphysical counterpart for that knowledge. By Soyinka's explication, it would seem that the ritual power of music not only invokes that connection, but also manifests, albeit fleetingly, the knowledge's *illud tempus* presence.

I have taken this concept further to suggest that any individual's serious commitment to the sound of music—most especially by way of church hymnal, gospel, jazz, organ voluntary, piano concerto—is a ritual attempt to connect with his or her spirituality, an attempt to evoke or regain the nature of the original oneness in the *illud tempus*. It is an experience, I propose, that is at once nostalgic of the separation and joyful of the union. It is within the intensity of the experience that whatever knowledge sought manifests. I have also undertaken to define the experience in terms of the creative artist and playwright's creative process which, similarly, describes a confrontation with spirituality, the playwright's spirituality. It is the playwright's inner voice, in need of a creative/dramatic idea, that emerges from the depths to make a metaphysical connection in the playwright's psyche. In the intensity of the experience, an idea-note strikes, and is sustained, at first as a monotone; then, through continued ritual immersion, the idea eventually manifests an *illud tempus* script.

The concept is not really farfetched. We need only consider the probable ritual beginnings of Western theater identified by the dithyramb and the chorus dancers. We can deduce that the dithyramb is an improvisational expression that begins with a song invocation, and with the song and dance the presence of Dionysus, the godhead of the chorus' spirituality, or individuality, becomes manifest. The chorus seeks a common goal—to find meaning for their communal fate in the material world or, in Yoruba terms, to connect with a presence identified as their metaphysical counterpart through whom they can define their communal fate and within it their individual fate. The experience can also be likened to a church worship with songs and sometimes dance, in which God is called upon, both in anguish and elation, to help direct the congregational fate in which their individual fates on earth participate. Similarly, we can connect the development of European theater after the Dark Ages to its spiritual origins in the medieval church.[4] In fact, it can be stated that religious experiences are the basis of contemporary Western theater.

Through a similar connection and experience in the playwright's *illud tempus* or psyche, a dramatic idea is born. Through ritual immersions, to which the playwright submits with the total trust of his or her creative resources of interpretation, that idea develops into a playscript. Really this intuitive rendering is true for any psychic transmission. Even then, the expression with its message, though an accurate interpretation, must at first be seen as a tentative vision of the individual, which thereafter must be shaped objectively by an understanding of form. Furthermore, the interpretation needs an audience with a common empathic support, or a religious bind, just as gods need the support of their devotees. And, perhaps, here lies the tragedy of humankind. For any given vision is limited, and much as its interpretation aims to relate to the generality, it cannot hope to capture or affect the totality of human experience, only shades and segments of it. Therefore the individual with his or her interpretation and message must expect to please and displease. But let us proceed with the rest of the question posed: What is the nature of the idea?

As a dramatic idea or note coded with language (word, music, gestures) and images, it is pertinent to say that the idea is a compact raw form of the play later to be fleshed out more concretely—in other words, the idea contains all the ingredients or components of a play. These components are engaged in a process similar to that of ritual, that is, they describe a need (to combat a crisis), a sacrifice (that such combat demands) and an efficacy (that achieves or does not achieve the need). To make comparisons of these components in ritual and drama more effectively, we should first explore the progression of a ritual process as a common structure in art and, in fact, in all human experiences.

Everything in nature, be it human or element, has what can be identified in its development as a beginning, a middle and an end. But what is the nature of that beginning, that middle, and that end? Knowledge of that nature is crucial to anyone whose need it is to create, so that the process can be implemented at will. As it is crucial to a farmer to understand the growth of crops, so it is crucial for the artist to understand the developmental process of his or her art in order to facilitate creations, or re-creations. Here, the word *recreation* may arrest our curiosity. Often used nonchalantly to mean a moment to pass the time in between some routine jobs, chores or duties, upon reconsideration, it suggests a more specific meaning, fruitful with information. It suggests a resting or contemplating mode in which we are able to confront our spirituality—the totality of our individuality—in order to be able to create afresh, that is, with meaningful strategies that implicate our survival in a complex world of different interacting fates, and of crises. While the repetitive act of re-creation, or resting, conforms with the surface understanding of ritual, the process of development, whether for art or for survival, should be understood as the progression-phases of the ritual process we have identified. It is to these we must now direct our attention, and then use relevant plays to identify them more practically.

NEED

The first phase of a ritual process is, of course, whatever need requires to be done—the purpose, the objective. Various suggestions have been offered as the need for humankind to be on earth or, implicating the source itself, the purpose of God's creation or manifestation. For those who ritually create and re-create in one medium or another, this matter is particularly intriguing. But whatever that purpose is, it would seem to be described by the way each individual deals with the continual need for survival. We can never know exactly why we are created or the purpose of human existence, unless we speculate. But the act of survival, through eating, working, accumulating wealth, praying and so forth, presents the various reasons for living. These visual expressions of living, in fact, would seem to discourage any need to torture our imagination for further explanations, except to satisfy our insatiable curiosity. Indeed, the multiple needs, as each manifests, are enough to give us an idea of the complex nature of creation and of the ritual mysteries of creativity. Our human attitude to the needs, simply, could be described as the necessity to live or, simpler still, the necessary curiosity to investigate, experience and understand anything that the earth and living offer—be it beauty, ugliness, danger, love, hate, hope, despair, wealth, poverty—in short, all the fateful and fatal encounters that come our way either to challenge, or to confirm our reasons for being and for wishing to be.

By contemplating the needs to understand and to survive, we have come upon possible subjects for a play, and as playwrights, we may further investigate their dramatic potential. In other words, these abstractions, or ideas that have struck the psyche, need to be given concrete and visible forms, so that they can be better understood. The process of giving an idea form also begins the racking and the development of the playwright's sense of imagination and invention.

Let us consider the common but very difficult concept *love*, common because it is one of the most explored and exploited words in the English language, but difficult because it is a deceptive, even elusive, emotion, one whose expression is problematic and has caused many misunderstandings, acute anxiety and heart-wrenching disappointments. The artist-playwright, in order to understand the nature of the idea of love, would probably wish to define the word as evocatively and concretely as possible. This can be done in at least two ways. The playwright may decide to use the narrative form by creating a story that conveys the meaning, or the descriptive form which tries to realize the meaning concretely. Whichever choice, the exercise requires the artist-playwright to paint pictures of love with words. For example:

> *Narrative Form*: A Caucasian American who has been buried in an earthquake disaster for several hours sees the light of day as he is pulled out of the debris by his African-American co-victim of accident. Or,
> There, amid the terror and the confusion of the hurricane, her nest caught between the branches of a pine tree, a bird enfolds her two babies in her wings.
> *Descriptive Form*: Sunrise breaking the clouds over the dewy mountains in vermillion rays of a favorable day. Or,
> Pink flamingos flap dance in the light rain on the shores of their habitat-river.

Taking into consideration the fact that one person's creative preference is another's instinctive repulsion, everyone does not have to agree with the examples. In fact, it is important that each person's picture or image is his or her own. Creativity should reflect the creator's individuality—a factor of spirituality that makes us all different, even though, as is often the case, we might be linked by common interests that make communal spirituality possible. The exercise is not as easy as it seems, even with a common word like *love*, hence the idea in the psyche compels a great deal of concentration and sincerity.

If we achieve the objective, we may, charged by a dramatic sense of curiosity, go on to explore an antonymic concept of the word, *hate*, so that we have a contrasting picture. This would be useful later on in the expression being developed from the idea, especially considering that playwriting, more than other performed arts, indulges in battle of opposites, which creates intense conflicts. Indeed, the interpretive, ritual power of an artist (really, of any person)) comprises both positive and negative forces, which characterize the individual's potential (and this is demonstrated fully by the concept of artists' potential) as, at once, creative and destructive.

Need, the first component of ritual, begins to focus the idea or note that strikes the playwright's psyche—the need to love, or the need of love, for which sacrifices must be made. It is the subject-key, so to speak, that strikes the note or idea. The key strikes, vibrating dramatic possibilities.

SACRIFICE

Do all ritual enactments go through sacrifice? A colleague of mine once posed the legitimate question against my ritual process construct. The question can be counterposed by another: Do all needs require some form of sacrifice?

To begin with, we should think of an act of sacrifice beyond its more common but restrictive meaning, which often reflects some pain and suffering. But then pain or suffering also requires a broader definition. A need, be it as commonplace as wanting to write to a friend, as practical as needing a car, or as emotional (and as exploitative) as desiring sex, requires a certain amount of effort to fulfill. Within that effort is some level or form of pain, whether in looking for the writing materials, or in engaging in an act of writing, or in choosing an automobile to purchase among various makes and to fit a particular budget, or in attaining a level of emotional state for both partners that would make intercourse not only possible but also enjoyable.

Sacrifice, in these examples, assumes a broader meaning—the act giving oneself over in an effort to realize a particular objective, which may result in success or failure. Any of these acts of sacrifice anticipates the success of the effort, otherwise such an act of sacrifice may not be necessary. However, the need to engage in the act of sacrifice, if we care to think about it, presupposes possible handicaps—which are really a source of pain because they frustrate the effort of the objective, raising conflict because the success of the objective is in doubt. It is possible, for instance, that a pencil or pen is not nearby and has to be found, and even if found, does not function properly, so that another one has to be found or bought. If locating paper, pen or pencil is easy enough, not so might what exactly to write about, or the right word or phrase to convey an emotional thought. As for trying to buy a car, just the thought of dealing with car salesmen can cause anxiety. And in terms of sex, one can encounter a host of complications, both comical and tragical, in trying to initiate, let alone achieve the desired pleasure. Sitcoms, such as *Seinfeld*, are littered with examples of such situations.

Although the stuff of conflict does not concern us at the moment, it is inevitable to mention it discussing sacrifice, which implicates objective, effort, conflict, and the pain caused by that conflict. In fact, we can see how the idea that strikes the creative psyche begins to develop, through the ritual paradigm, with some of the crucial elements of drama, namely, the crisis, the objective, the conflict, and, in the third stage of progression, the denouement:

EFFICACY

Efficacy is the end phase of the ritual progression. It is the result or the outcome of the need through sacrifice—which every objective anticipates. A general misunderstanding often associated with the condition is that the outcome necessarily denotes success, but the outcome of the objective is successful only in the sense that it is realized. The objective itself could either fail or succeed; the need desired by a person or a community may or may not be met, despite the sacrifice or sacrifices made. For instance, in a traditional ritual where the need is for rain so that food crops could grow, animal sacrifices would be made to placate the respective powers; rain might come and there is an end to the famine, but it might not and famine continues. If the famine continues, the objective obviously did not succeed, and the outcome might be attributed to a divine source who still needed to be approached to gain knowledge of his intention. Thus, the priest questing on behalf of his community would continue to seek other sacrifices so that it might rain.

A play works in a similar fashion. The central need is achieved only after the central character makes a sacrifice, or a series of sacrifices. But the difference between a traditional ritual and a theater "ritual" lies in time, that linear measurement that defies or tries to compartmentalize the natural process. A play, as defined in the Western world, is framed within a constructive time limit, in which we must learn whether or not the need/objective was achieved for whatever dramatic reasons the playwright suggests.

The playwright, by virtue of his or her questing, also describes a ritual need with the idea that struck, and while we are on the success or failure of an objective, we should note that this also applies to the playwright. The objective of the playwright to write a play—an attempt to flesh out a ritual idea concerning *love, jealousy, hope,* or *isolation*—may, or may not be achieved, even though the play is fully expressed. In other words, the playwright may, or may not have conveyed his or her ritual interpretation, the message, successfully to his or her audience, the community for whom the play is written. It is also possible that the playwright's interpretation of the idea is muddled and therefore runs counter to the expectations of his or her audience.

Indeed, we have traveled a roundabout route to begin to understand the initial phase of the creative process, the playwright's quest to broach the *illud tempus* on behalf of the community/audience. Through a ritual engagement with the mythic powers, the Muses of the playwright, an idea strikes, an idea coded with messages in sound and images. The idea, an emanation of the mythic powers, also contains the ritual/dramatic structure through which the playwright will physically interpret and express the psychic idea. While the process also occurs in other creative arts, in playwriting the ritual receives its fullest expression, since it not only anticipates dramatization of the present (imagined truth) and the presence (of physical events) that theater makes, but also incorporates the ingredients of the other creative art forms (visual art, poetry, music, etc.).

The interpretation however depends on the acute vision of the playwright/quester, and his or her tonal resource, that is, his or her voice—the ritual power of re-creation and imagination. It is the single factor of language that links the playwright directly to music. The voice of the playwright is the physical extension of his or her muse-ic, which is expressed, first in what I call a monotonic monologue, and subsequently in dialogue—Chapter 5 will consider more fully the "monotone" with which the playwright engages the idea into a multi-tonal dramatic expression. But in case there is any doubt about this monotonic engagement, consider the Greek origins of Western theater, beginning with the choric song and dance of the mythic idea, which Thespis, as the first actor/playwright, adopted and then used his vocal power to intone and interpret, constituting the "monotone" of his monologue. In much the same way, but with much more evocative elaboration, Soyinka sets the tonal language of Yoruba tragedy within the ritual power of music. In an effort to bridge the cosmic chasm, the soul-wrenching chant of the "possessed lyricist . . . (in) mythopoeic strains . . . is . . . caught and thrust with all its terror and awesomeness into the night by swaying votaries . . ."[5] What then is the nature of the playwright's voice, this medium of his spirituality, the ritual power associated with music?

Consider the pipe-organ, that king of musical instruments, whose ritual potential in my estimation has yet to be formally determined, even though it has been the basis of mood, thematic or incidental sound to many dramas (silent movies, musicals, plays, etc.). At its basest, its timbre could be very profound, at its most climactic, its full tones could be cathartically therapeutic and awe-inspiring, but its power could also assume a middle tonal quality that is mystifying, serene and quintessential.[6] It is no coincidence that the ritual power of this instrument should be felt most profoundly in an establishment where individuals (singly or communally) probe their spirituality. To be sure, its dramatic resources have been exploited to some extent in musicals such as *The Phantom of the Opera*, and by pop simulations of them, such ultimately commercial ventures have in fact vibrated back to the spirituality of the evangelical church, albeit with their commercial aspect. However, exploring and verifying the presence of these resources within the context of drama should enlighten us about the nature of their power and, by connection, open up more creative possibilities for the playwright.

Let us recall a moment in Shakespeare's *The Tempest*. Prospero, through his spirit-servant, has been torturing the minds of Prospero's culprits, to bring them to the awareness of the crime they committed, especially his brother, Alonzo, who deviously usurped the crown of Spain from him. Racked by Ariel's soul-searching monologue, Alonzo admits his guilt in a harrowing anguish:

> O, it is monstrous, monstrous!
> Methought the billows spoke and told me of it,
> The winds did sing it to me; and the thunder,
> That deep and dreadful *organ pipe*, pronounced (my emphasis)
> The name of Prosper: it did bass my trespass.
> (Act 3, sc.3, lines 95—99)[7]

Whether Shakespeare was aware of it or not, the speech evokes its anguish through the compelling power of the "organ pipe," whose "deep and dreadful" sound rises from the bowels, its bellows, to indict and torture the minds of Alonzo and his men to the awareness "of sin" committed, preparing them for the efficacious need of atonement. This response with its evocation of the pipe organ sound, inevitably recalls the speech that compels it—Ariel's monologic denouncement of the criminals—the very "organ pipe." If we take a look at it, we will find that all the tonal and metaphoric images in the monologue are efficacious projections that are dramatized and realized in the play—the anger of the "never-surfeited sea," that belches up humans; the "ministers of Fate" on Prospero's island that have manipulated the conscience of the criminals with guilt; and the anticipated restorative resonance of "a clear life ensuring."[8]

It becomes evident, therefore, that Ariel's speech is not only the source of Alonzo's anguish and repentance, but also the ritual voice/power of the "organ pipe." In fact, if we study the monologue, we can find in it all the phases of the ritual process we have mentioned (the need, the sacrifice, and the efficacy), which Alonzo not only echoes but also describes as a lead victim. The organ-like sound of the storm that "bass (his) trespass" leads Alonzo to an act of desperate repentance and redemption, first making him to seek his son to lower depths "than e'er the plummet sounded/ And with him there lie mudded."[9] It is a sacrifice we know, through Ariel, is worthy of "a clear life ensuring."

Reconsidering the organ-recitative of Ariel's monologue, the ritual tonality and modality, therefore the ritual power of the pipe organ, become more apparent. We must keep in mind that the power of the storm is metaphorically likened to the power of the organ. In fact, there is no single musical instrument, that I know of, that can most effectively capture or evoke the powerful sound of an ocean-storm for us, such as is implied in the monologue and Shakespeare's *Tempest*.

The first part of the speech establishes the indictment, the deep resonance of a crisis that will force the need to seek atonement:

> You are three men of sin, whom Destiny,
> That hath to instrument this lower world
> And what is in't, the never-surfeited sea
> Hath caused to belch up you.
> Act 3-3, lines 53–56

The speech then goes on to relate this action to the incident of crime, in which the criminals

> From Milan did supplant good Prospero,
> Exposed unto the sea, which hath requit it,
> Him and his innocent child; for which foul deed,
> The powers, delaying, not forgetting, have
> Incensed the seas and shores, yea all the creatures
> Against your peace.
> Act 3-3, lines 70–75

On the surface the reminder might seem unnecessary and long-winded, but we must remember its purpose: to bring the criminals to awareness through suffering, with words and phrases that incites and indicts:

> You fools! I and my fellows
> Are ministers of Fate—the elements,
> Of whom your swords are tempered may as well
> Wound the loud winds, or with bemocked-at stabs
> Kill the still-closing waters, as diminish
> One dowl that's in my plume. My fellow ministers
> Are like invulnerable.
> Act 3-3, lines 60–68

The incitement challenges the futile resistance of the captured criminals, frozen-up with drawn swords that are "too massy for your strengths/ And will not be uplifted" (lines 67–68). It also suggests the ineffectuality of the crime committed—"The powers" (Prospero's), delayed since he and his daughter's survival on the island, now levy just punishment "(a)gainst your peace." Notice also how the seeming circumlocution, indeed the constant flow and ebb of the breaking sea, has been emphasized by the punctuation, and the difficult rhythm and line-breaks of the verse. In short, it is a weighty crime deserving a weighty punishment being acknowledged by the monologue; the ultimate objective of forgiveness is therefore difficult. Musically, it is like the changing modes of the organ-sound, effected through counterpoint and the pulling and the shutting of the stops.

The climax of the sacrificial sequence comes with a deserving punishment: a "Ling'ring perdition, worse than any death/ Can be at once" (lines 77–78).[10] It is a fatal penalty that is tempered however with a fateful vision of forgiveness, "a clear life ensuing," attained through Alonzo's atonement. The efficacy of this ritual experience will be Alonzo's agonized self-recognition.

The speech is an example of how the playwright, wittingly or unwittingly, has used music-coded words. To effect the full impact of Ariel's "organ pipe" recitative, the monologue needs complementary backing of sound, and in this case no sound is more appropriate than that of the organ. It is essential, however, that this accompaniment, in order to create its effect, should be in the background, since the venom of Ariel's speech is in the organ-powered words—the organ underscore should remain a rumbling reminder of the tempest. It is also important to note that the anger remains in the lower depths of the ocean, and does not really erupt. The eruption happened in the recent past, at the beginning of the play when the "never-surfeiting sea" was "caused to belch up" the victims. In the monologue, the anger is suppressed, only recalled in the murmur of words and sound. In this regard, the organ accompaniment evocatively ritualizes the implications of the speech. How then can the playwright benefit from the resources of the organ sound?

Just as words, speeches, or an entire play can be coded with music, so can a piece of music—be it classical, jazz or rock—be coded with word images. In other words, emotions, feelings or thoughts evoked by a piece of music can be expressed in words. For instance, to be able to express emotions raised by sounds from an organ, and therefore experience its ritual power, we will have to listen to organ recitals, or the harmonies of improvising virtuosos at the organ—the public radio, for instance, has featured the music and recitals of such organists.[11] Exercises, developed to capture images of the ritual power of sound, may bring creative rewards. However, such exercises are not limited to the organ music. Piano and violin concertos, or jazz renditions, for instance, or any favorite music choice of any individual for that matter, are good for evoking ideas and images of the creative/ritual process. Furthermore, much use can be made of abstract visual art, such as painting or sculpture, to elicit the imaginative response of students.[12]

But more pertinent to our understanding of the creative/ritual process, is the attitude of the playwright/quester to the idea-note that strikes in the playwright's psyche—that is, the particular interpretation of a particular playwright in the development of his or her script. This can be likened to the attitude of the high-priest/shaman to a received response from the *illud tempus* for his community. Since it is possible for creative personages (organist, pianist, dancer, visual artist, etc.) to attain the psychic experience, the attitude is not limited to the playwright. In the theater alone, the attitude not only relates to the playwright, but also to the director and the actor as creative artists. Similarly, in the play itself, we can talk about the experience of the central character and his or her attitude to the situation being expressed, and, in a scene or a unit, we can consider the central focus of the scene or unit and the character's attitude to the situation. How then do we represent the attitude of the playwright?

The complexity of the expressions that make up the creative process—a network of shifting perspectives—can be demonstrated clearly with the playwright's expression, the *illud tempus* script. First, the authorial voice of the psychic experience, the playwright's, shifts to the central character of the expressed idea, which in its physical expression on stage must also shift to the actor through the director. But within the script, we can also talk about the shifting points of view of the authorial voice, from the central focus of one scene to another. For instance, with Ariel's recitative, we see Ariel (acting on behalf of Prospero) as the priest/artist of Alonzo's atonement in the ritual space of the island. The complex network of attitudes points to the complex psyche of the playwright, the high priest/quester or the "possessed lyricist" of the idea-note that struck in the *illud tempus*.

But this explanation of the shifting perspectives of authorial voice necessitates a clarification. Let us reconsider the example made with Ariel, in order to justify the organ sound that counterpoints his recitative. Since music is an artistic expression by right, with its own artistic source and artist-quester, the application of organ sound would seem to query or contradict our implication of Ariel as the surrogate high priest of the evocation of restorative repentance. However, in this instance, as we have no knowledge of any physical source of the sound other than Ariel, it remains an abstract force which Ariel uses to support and direct his indictment, in order to effect Prospero's objective. We can argue that Prospero uses Ariel because of his capacity for that music resource, although it is also possible to argue that Prospero's power provides Ariel with that capacity—which is doubtful, considering the fact that Prospero is dependent on Ariel's fulfillment of his objective. Consistent with other sounds in the play used by Ariel, the organ sound can be justified as an abstract power at Ariel's command, even though he acts on behalf of Prospero. In fact, it is part of the ritual power (or muse-ic) of Ariel, the surrogate high priest, who at once interprets and evokes the need for atonement with his power of words and music. Furthermore by our analysis, we may say that Ariel's words are the concretized form of the abstract music-coded idea, which Ariel employs on behalf of Prospero—just as the actor interprets the drama of the playwright, whose visionary experience in ideational sounds and responses in the *illud tempus* has primally realized the idea-note that strikes first in monologic, and then expresses itself in dialogic terms. Hence, Ariel serves as both the surrogate and the source. This, in fact, would seem to make an argument for the actor, who also, although acts on behalf of the playwright, uses his own intuitive powers to interpret the character of the playwright. And, perhaps, it is this capacity that differentiates a virtuoso or a star from an ordinary artist or actor,[13] and therefore ultimately justifies Cole's perception of the "role-possessed body and embodied role"of the actor as primal artist.[14]

Through the example of Ariel and *The Tempest*, it should be evident that music is an important part of the idea-note that strikes the psyche. This idea, the muse-ic of the creative process is coded with various sounds that the playwright/artist must decode, interpret and express in dialogue, visual images, incidental sounds etc. Thus, for musical sound to serve visually as an evocative dramatic resource, we need to understand its nature and its source by which we are able locate the quester of the creative process (playwright, central character, actor) and, perhaps, the community for whom he or she is questing. In African music, for instance, the ritual dancer can interpret the tonal messages encoded in the emphatic tones of the leading "mother" drum. These tones, on the other hand, are the attitude of the quester/interpreter/drummer to the idea-note that struck, that is, the received response from the *illud tempus*—the source of the ritual power of the creative process. Similarly, in a singing chorale, the leading voice of the chorus intones or interprets the received response of the creator of the song or cantata. In Western music, instruments such as organ, violin, cello, and piano similarly can characterize the power of the ritual process. In these instances, the artist (drummer, choral leader, organist, violinist, cellist, pianist) is the high-priest/interpreter of an expressed psychic idea. These artists, however, may well be primal questers (like the playwright, composer or improviser), or surrogates who interpret on behalf of the primal artist/quester (like an actor), or they could in fact be both (like a virtuoso). Whatever the case, we must understand their different artistic function in relation to the metaphysical process, and their different attitude to the idea that strikes. They are all questing artists, by right. But while the primal artist quests the *illud tempus* from where he or she receives the idea, the surrogate quests the *illud-tempus* script, and the virtuoso traverses both ritual arenas. The psychical experience of most creative artists seems to fall within these three modes and spaces. However, as questers of their various creative space, they are all driven by similar objectives—to make efficacious a "need," through "sacrifice." They are also questing for the needs of their community, audiences or listeners, who are supposed to be in receipt of not only the questers' interpretation but also a therapeutic catharsis—the efficacy of "a clear life ensuring."

To reiterate, the purpose, objective or "need" in this chapter is to attempt to crystallize for the creative writer, especially the playwright, the nature of his or her creative process in order to widen the scope of the artist's creative resources. It is a creative quest that racks the psyche, sacrificially, for ideas and for the expression of those ideas. The set of exercises in the Appendix is designed to help the playwright enter his or her creative space, be alert to the idea-note that strikes, the muse-ic (idea, voice, power)with which the playwright ritually engages his or her psyche into developing a dramatic expression.

NOTES

1. Cole, *Theatrical Event*, 7–11; Mircea Eliade, *Shamanism: Archaic Techniques of Esctasy*, trans. Willard R. Trask (Princeton: Princeton University Press, 1972).

2. For short summary of the ritual experiments of these theater groups, see Arthur Sainer, *The New Radical Theatre Notebook*, New, Expanded, Revised Edition (New York: Applause, 1997), chapters 3, 8 and 14.

3. *Myth, Literature and the African World*, Appendix: "The Fourth Stage,"145–149.

4. For the development of theatre in Medieval Europe, see Oscar Brockett, *History of Theatre*, 9th edition (MA: Allyn and Bacon, 1999), ch.4.

5. *Myth, Literature*, 148–149.

6. Various classical works demonstrate the dramatic resources of the pipe organ. For example: Camille Saint-Saens' symphony No. 3: *Organ Symphony*.

7. William Shakespeare, *The Tempest*, ed. Stephen Orgel (Oxford:Clarendon Press, 1987), 169.

8. For Ariel's monologue, see *Tempest*, 166–168.

9. *Tempest*, 169.

10. *Tempest*, 167.

11. For instance, recitals of Philip Langlais, and one of his favorite pupil, Haji Hakim, both of whom have been featured in *Pipedreams*: programs Nos. 0127 and 0130 (Minnesota: Public Radio, July 2001).

12. See exercises in "Appendix I."

13. The use of the word, "star" is limited to the stage recognition of it, not to the more general usage in the movie business.

14. *Theatrical Event*, 5.

Chapter Two

Mythic Expressions of the Creative Process: *The Fateful/Fatal Paradox*

All artists feel the need to create, but what to create at any particular moment of the creative process may be elusive at first. A playwright feels the need to write a play, but then what play? Even if the playwright has conceived an idea, having an idea or a situation does not make a play, which still has to be written. Thus, the playwright, like any other creative artist, initially faces an abyss—there are so many possibilities, but none that is yet conceivable. This abyss is the amorphous or chthonic world the playwright must invade, and like his or her divine archetypes (the Greek Dionysus, and the Yoruba Ogun) the playwright must experience the fateful/fatal challenges of his or her creative process—the psychical forces that incite, or strike, the idea or note, and the physical forces the playwright must use to explore and express the idea. As stated, idea-note represents the inspiration, the 1 or 2 percent of the creative process, the rest of which requires both inventive and physical effort for any expression to materialize.

The playwright must come to terms with these forces of expression to be able to perceive dramatically what the idea-note constitutes. This attitude of the playwright, a struggle to crack, as it were, a kernel of an idea, is at once ritual and dynamic. In this chapter, we shall examine the ritual process with already written texts that present obvious dramatic explorations of the fate of the central character. For most plays, ultimately, is about the fate the central character or characters. These texts, we must bear in mind, have not only undergone the ritual process, in terms of grounding an idea, of the exploration of that idea, and of actual expression of the idea. They have subsequently stood the test of interpretation in their ritual bind with performance, and with audience receptivity.

Lest the exercise should follow the path of literary criticism, we must endeavor to continue to hold the dramatic text in the ritual context we have been considering—the text as an emanation of a ritual challenge and struggle, an expression of the idea-note struck in the creative psyche. This perception in fact takes us back to reconsider the components of ritual, and their implications to the experience of the playwright. While acknowledging the already established structure of a ritual process as paradigmatic of the structural components of the idea and of the dramatic text itself, we cannot but wonder and be curious about the ritual affinities of the text, the substance of the playwright's expression. In other words, how may we define this substance in ritual terms?

We can seek an understanding by considering the substance of ritual itself, which we can suggest as mythic by the fact of Northop Frye's recognition of myth as a narrative of ritual[1]. Since the process of ritual is dramatic, may we not conclude that the narrative, the expressive content of ritual, myth, is also dramatic? Therefore, if ritual is drama and that drama is mythic, may we not also conclude that the "narrative" expression of drama (the story that makes drama) is mythic?

This takes us back to the ritual beginnings of theater, which consist of enactments of the myths of gods Isis and Osiris; Dionysus, the Greek patron of the arts; and, later, Christ in the Medieval church. Semblances of such rituals still can be located in traditional cultures of Asia and Africa. In fact, when we talk about drama as literary texts, it is possible to discuss them as re-creation of myths, especially those written by our Greek authors and the modern recreations of their plays.

It can be argued, in fact, that drama, from its inception and by its ritual affinities, has always been an expression of myth. Apart from the fact that the idea struck in the psyche may have generated from fiction, such as with Shakespeare, any drama can be argued to be fictive, by the very nature of the idea-note that struck. For the idea—whether induced by myth or fiction or, as is prevalent in our day, by real personal experiences—and the expression that develops from it, are very much an individual's or a set of individuals' notion of the nature of things. Since what is reality for one individual is probably fiction for another, any person's idea as to the nature of things can be considered fictive, regardless of the fact that there are basic social agreements and standards. For such norms, after all, derived from some people's opinions and then became established as workable mores for social and political stability of the community. Well may we wonder, why humankind is divided by so many systems such as communism, capitalism, democracy, Christianity, Islam, Buddhism, and so forth.

Furthermore, in fiction as in drama, we talk about the realism of an expression as opposed to the reality of things. This distinction makes a play a realistic articulation of an experience in dramatic form, as opposed to a real experience, if indeed there is such a thing. Thus, because of the nature of its expression, drama, especially as realized in performance, has constantly dealt with and has variously exploited the inherent problematic differences of reality and illusion. Two plays that immediately come are Luigi Pirandello's *Six Characters in Search of an Author*,[2] or Jean Paul Satre's *No Exit*.[3] In the humanistic world view of *Six Characters*, we are forced to question whose reality we are supposed to take—the "real" actors who are trying to create an illusion of reality, or the fictional characters whose presence participates in the reality of their actions. In *No Exit*, Sartre presents the living "hell" we create for ourselves when we determine our "real" character through the distorted image, the illusion, of how we allow others to perceive us—the tormenting illusion in which we become hopelessly caught through fictive construct of ourselves.

If we accept the mythic conceptions of drama and theater, and that these conceptions express the narrative content of drama, we should be able to establish more firmly the ritual implications of that content by drawing attention to another fact of ritual evident within drama. It is the fact that, ultimately, all ritual enactment—whether in honor of a god or ancestor, whether in the form of a prayer, a song or a dance, or whether by the mass media persistent call for the release of American hostages in Iraq—has to do with a certain fate, often that of an individual or a group of individuals. By ritual affinities, we can say that most, if not all creative expressions, particularly performative expressions such as drama, have to do with a certain fate of the central focus, whether imposed directly through the artist's point of view as frequently occurs in visual art and poetry, or indirectly through a character or characters in a play or dance or epic poetry. Both imposed points of view can be seen in the creative process of playwriting, where the playwright not only focuses an objective with a central character but imposes his or her own character and opinion on the fictive character. It is this fate that needs to be imaged with its bearer from the idea that struck, one way or another (partially or fully), before any physical expression can begin to manifest.

With this in mind, let us consider the complex, fateful/fatal nature of the relationship between the fate of the central character, and the playwright's commitment to it. We shall start with the two plays already suggested as more obvious dramas about fate, *Oedipus Rex* and *Waiting for Godot*; then move on to the less obvious in Shakespeare's *Othello*, and three one-acts, Edward Albee's *The Zoo Story*, LeRoi Jones' *Dutchman* and Sam Shepard's *A Fool for Love*. These plays will be assessed from the point of view of the author, as if the author is engaged in the creative process in the present, coming up with an idea, and with the choices to realize that idea. Of course, we will never know exactly how any of the playwrights conceived his play, even if we heard such a process straight from the horse's mouth, usually after the fact. We can only suggest what might have happened as a demonstration of this ritual concept of playwriting, an attempt to give expression to the creative engagement that begins in the playwright's psyche.

Sophocles, we know, created *Oedipus Rex* from a myth that focuses on the fate of Oedipus. Dogged from childhood by the prediction that he would kill his father and marry his mother, Oedipus tried to escape from that fate, only to learn too late that he still had to confront the already realized fate. In that sense, we could say the idea-note that struck Sophocles was that paradox of fate, the fateful/fatal complex that seemed to have molded Oedipus' individuality—Sophocles recalled this from within the mythic premises of Oedipus' genealogy and Greek cosmology. The narrative idea, even though it possesses dramatic tension—a man confronted by the fate he is running away from—at this stage is not the drama Sophocles wrote. Knowledge of his intention came to him through the ritual struggle of questing in his psyche. Looking at the drama he finally expresses, we gain an understanding of that struggle, that is, the choices he must have made and imposed on his central character. Yet, judging by the initial response I usually get in my playwriting class, the fact of the choices can be somewhat misleading.

As indicated earlier most students first identify the subject or focus of the play as the fate of Oedipus. True enough, but what fate? Usually, the students mean the fate suggested by Sophocles' source, the narrative idea—running from fate and being confronted by it. But is that fate central to the play? Where in the play does Oedipus run from his fate only to confront it, that is, aside from the stirrings provoked or awakened in his mind by Teiresias and Jocasta, or apart from the information delivered by the messenger from Corinth? What a play is about concerns what actually happens in the play, the visible action as opposed to the expository information. It is within the visible action that we can track the real fate of Oedipus in the play.

Rather than the mythic fate of Oedipus, what is dramatized is the action taken by King Oedipus to validate his seemingly divine authority through solving riddles; in doing so, he comes to terms with who he really is, a fateful/fatal action that leads him to blind himself. In other words, *Oedipus Rex* is a play about establishing the truth of identities, and about the way Oedipus does this. In his attempt to describe this action—the dramatized fate as opposed to the mythic fate—Oedipus is confronted with obstacles (conflicts), the most significant being his own character, his egocentricism, which consists the character-traits such as pride, impulsiveness, rashness, and quickness to temper. Through these traits, and by Oedipus' reaction to other characters (other fates), external obstacles and conflicts arise—such as, the somewhat sadistic relish of Teiresias' exposition of Oedipus as the killer, the superficial restraint and the fickleness of Jocasta in trying to avoid telling the truth, and the arrogant self-aggrandizement of Creon to exonerate himself from Oedipus's accusation.

Classical Greek worldview warns us of the excess that reveals weakness in our otherwise strong fateful characters, the fatal blindness that characterizes our choice of direction and which propels our hubristic action to catastrophe Such action, especially demonstrated by good and prominent personages, is the stuff of tragedy, hence the tragic heroism of classical tragedy. The drama of Oedipus therefore seems to be a perfect example for Sophocles. Struck by the narrative idea, he wrestles with it, challenged by the tragic heroism Oedipus' character suggests, and which Sophocles chooses to express. Only the fate-action proposed by the character of Oedipus matters, although this action can only be realized effectively through its fateful/fatal confrontation with that of other characters, such as Creon and Teiresias. Their character traits are potential ingredients for Oedipus' hubristic drive and tragic heroism—what led to gorging his own eyes out. In fact, that visual and concrete image—eyes gorged out—so characteristic of Oedipus' impulsive character, might have emerged, first, from the idea that struck, which then gave birth to choice of characters and the way they pose obstacles to Oedipus' objective. Sophocles, with his penchant for strong characters and consistent with *Oedipus Rex*, would go on to explore the fate-action of other central characters confronted by with similar oppositional ingredients, such as those that confront Creon in *Antigone*—principally, the character traits of Antigone herself.

Oedipus Rex is about the fate of King Oedipus, not the mythic/divine fate that probably is our first instinctive choice, but the realistic/human, which becomes obvious when we consider the present time of the play. In the Yoruba world view, the difference between these kinds of fate-action is clear. The mythic/divine is the fate endowed in the metaphysical world of gods and ancestors, indeed chosen by the amorphous/embryonic entity of the unborn before birth. Perhaps it is the character-agent that completes the human form at birth—the Yoruba says that the god of fate and passage sanctions the chosen fate before the form passes into human existence. The realistic/human fate, on the other hand, is the expressed fate in the present world of the living, from life to death, sometimes differentiated by the word destiny.[4] One implies the objectified chosen, which fades into oblivion as the individual enters the life process; the other is the expressed impression of that choice, as it contends with life's obstacles and conflicts, through inevitable interrelationships with various fates or individuals. Although the physical individual struggles constantly, through telepathic connections with his or her metaphysical counterpart, to remember what was chosen, so as to channel himself or herself within its course, success very much depends on one's character, one's strengths and weaknesses in the survival process, indeed on one's hubristic action.[5] To this extent, everybody's fate has the tragic ingredient, which would also support Corrigan's notion that tragedy is generated by human as opposed to divine action.[6]

The realistic/human fate is usually what the playwright contends with, even if it initially might appear to be the mythic/divine, as it often seems with Greek dramatists. This is so, because the playwright must try to come to terms with life as it is lived in the present time of the play so as to engage his or her audience with the action dramatized. Through this struggle and action the playwright imposes his or her vision of the world. To this extent, it is a struggle that impacts the playwright's own fate. Oedipus' fate, to find the truth of established identities (of Laius and of himself), and the action he takes to do this, aligns with Sophocles' fate of giving expression to that truth and action as realistically as possible. One fate, Sophocles', becomes charged to express and realize the other, Oedipus', to its ultimate tragic consequence, which at its realization is diametrically related to the elation of Sophocles at the completion of his expression. On reflection though, the emotional response of author and central character to their respective accomplishments may be more alike than they appear. For, tragic heroism demands that the hero, in taking responsibility for his or her action, feels a sense of rapturous release, even in the face of catastrophic consequence.

Waiting for Godot, as I stated, also concerns the mythic/divine fate, perhaps more directly so than *Oedipus*, although there is a discernible thread of realistic/human fate. However, that mythic/divine fate, which originates from a mythic source, is dramatized as an idea, as opposed to an action describing a realistic/human fate. The realistic fate of Gogo and Didi, fashioned by an elusive (mythic?) character, Godot, is to wait for the coming of that mysterious character or entity to grant some favors. Both Gogo and Didi seem to have invested some faith in Godot on account of their tramp-like existence and situation, from which they seek change or some improvement. This is the siuation fleshed out from the idea-note that struck Beckett, and becomes expressed in the action of the idea.

To keep themselves from boredom and the anguish of the mythic fate of waiting for Godot to come, they engage in a realistic fate action that involves spontaneous or imposed activities, such as repartee, clowning, physical or mental exercise, mind-probing, and taking advantage of passersby. These endeavors, against the seemingly endless hours of their waiting, raise conflicts and a tragic fact. There is no certainty their waiting will realize their need— Godot may not come; therefore the favors they need may not be granted. Apparently they have been waiting for some time, and the present time of their waiting continues to yet another day, all to no avail. Even then, at the play's end, they decide to continue to wait. In fact, the hopelessness of the previous and probably subsequent fate-action of waiting, has brought despair and loss of faith, if only temporarily, to the point of suicide.

The hopelessness of hoping, or the fruitlessness of man's desire, is a tragic ingredient. This is the case with Gogo and Didi, despite the comical acts to which their fate-action commits them, in an effort to offset the thought of uncertainty. This tragic factor becomes even more emphatic when we realize that the fate-action of their persistent waiting is, ironically, also their worst hubristic enemy, that is, the way it seems to defy oppositions to it, oppositions such as the anguish of the waiting, Gogo's continual pessimism towards the endeavor, and, perhaps less directly, the glaring example of Lucky's situation as a hopeless case of perpetual servitude to his master, Pozzo, which is expressed both visually and verbally.

However, as in *Oedipus*, there is in *Waiting for Godot* a mythic/divine fate at play, the difference being that in *Waiting for Godot* the mythic fate is dramatized explicitly as an idea—in fact, an idea that seems to challenge or question the divine validity of the mythic fate. As such, the dramatized mythic/divine seems to be more important to the playwright than the action of the realistic/human, making it a play of ideas rather than one of action. Yet, both action and idea are well fused, so that we get intimations of the playwright's attitude to the mythic/divine within the expressed and dramatized fate-action—that is, his skeptical perception of the mythic/divine idea of salvation and damnation. Apparently, Beckett's source of this idea is a Saint Augustine's rather paradoxical, fateful/fatal palliative on salvation: "Do not despair; one of the thieves was saved. Do not presume; one of the thieves was damned."[7] It is the paradoxical idea that strikes Beckett, and which Beckett wishes to give dramatic development, a shape, with an objective that summarizes his own pessimistic position. Realizing and resolving the idea inherent in Saint Augustine's paradox as a dramatic expression is, therefore, Beckett's struggle with his own objective fate-action as a playwright.

First, he expresses the idea by allusions to the biblical story of the two thieves flanking Christ on the Cross.[8] It is probably the first image that concretizes the idea that struck. Then there is the situation of Pozzo and Lucky, the invaders of Gogo and Didi's (and the playwright's) ritual space, who seem to represent the privileged and the underdog, although both seem to be bound by a hopeless existence. Also, there is Lucky's recitative on the problem of existence,[9] and then, later on in the play, there is Pozzo's referent-image about the abysmal shortness of human existence, giving "birth astride of a grave" parroted a minute later by Didi[10]. More important, the mythic reality of the human condition and the objective graph Beckett describes with it are expressed by the seemingly hopeless objective action of Gogo and Didi, the fate described by their waiting.

The hopeful/hopeless situation of Gogo and Didi is compounded by their characteristic trait. Although they are tramps, and each displays his own peculiar character trait, we know from their repartee that they are quite witty, and intelligent. In fact, they display an impressive intellectual ability, which they sometimes throw off as comical circumstance, such as when Didi reminisces: "Hand in hand from the top of the Eiffel Tower, among the first. We were respectable in those days. Now it's too late. They wouldn't even let us up."[11] Sometime before, in their similar and complementary existence, it seems they had somehow diverted from their mythic-chosen fate of vocation, to the realized destiny conditioned by strategies of survival in the human world. It seems what they are now trying to do is to reintegrate their acquired realistic/human destiny with their mythic/chosen fate. This play, as should all plays, speaks very much to the plight of the human condition. Beckett, through the ritual rigors of his creative process, and informed by Saint Augustine's mythic/divine pronouncement, which Beckett places against a background of twentieth century experiences (war, capitalism, exploitation, isolation), imposes a comical but pessimistic point of view on the human condition—life is a joke, and salvation or survival is a fifty-fifty chance. This is the thematic idea, wrestled from the idea-note that struck, that forms the basis of Beckett's expression.

Shakespeare's *Othello* also describes such a tragic fate of the human condition, in terms of Othello's character and action. Present in most Shakespeare's plays, especially the tragedies, is the idea of the unaccommodated man, which King Lear reflects on when, rejected by his daughters, he confronts the raging storm outside and within him.[12] Following the classical theory of Aristotle on tragedy (and he has plays such as *Oedipus Rex* in mind), this idea is strongly dramatized with tragic heroes as they pit themselves against odds. Usually noble and basically good personages (i.e. not extremely good or bad), the heroes' characters are, however, flawed by the dominant human drive to survive, which limits their otherwise sound vision or judgment. We find this characteristic fateful/fatal flaw even in humanistic drama such as *The Tempest*. My reading of the play makes me conclude that Prospero in spite of, or because of his power seems to be consumed by a ruthless drive to manipulate, suppress and take revenge—that is, until his servant Ariel leads him to the possibility of accommodation and compassion:

> ARIEL ....
>   Your charms so strongly works 'em,
> That if you now beheld them, your affections
> Would become tender.
>
> PROSPERO.   Dost thou think so, spirit?

ARIEL.
Mine would, sir, were I human
(Act 5, sc.1, lines 17–19)[13]

Along with this basic classical concept, Shakespeare's plays are rooted in and are dramatized with the rich resources of his time, including cultural history, myths, documented romance, political schemes and scandals, and seasonal festivals. All these provide sources for the idea-notes that struck his psyche, evolving into a drama that is inventive, tragic and humorous, highly imagistic, and boisterously colloquial—indeed a treasury of Renaissance and universal resources. With these in mind, let us consider *Othello* in the fateful/fatal ritual context of the playwright's dramatic vision.[14] Without getting too much into the various approaches of literary criticism to the play, we can surmise Shakespeare's probable preoccupations, based on what the play's content reveals. The primary objective here is try and exemplify the thought process of a practicing playwright in the expression of his or her play.

Othello is Shakespeare's only play in which the central character is a black man, so we may fairly assume that the idea and theme of the black man's survival in an alien world crossed the playwright's mind or, at best, teased his creative psyche, begging investigation. It was certainly not the only time Shakespeare was or would be thus preoccupied, judging by other prominent black characters in his plays—Aaron in *Titus Andronicus* and Caliban in *The Tempest*.[15] The question is how can one effectively dramatize such an idea or vision, and what might the author's objective be in a world of survival full of complex possibilities that may impact the image of the black? To focus a respectable noble black in such a world must take enormous risks, since contemporary cultural impressions of the black man were hardly complimentary. Not that a story about a noble black man was not possible, or had not been heard of. On the contrary, in addition to the dominant impressions of the black man as a savage and a cannibal, stories abound of the noble black (although the idea of black nobility was often derogatory and patronizing) as well as phantasmagoric tales of blackness, in literature and from various reports by adventurers to exotic places for trade.[16] Whatever the case may be, such impressions must be considered more mythic than realistic, somewhat complimenting the mostly menial existence of blacks in Renaissance Europe.[17]

Some such stories, read by some playwright, could strike an idea-note that vibrates with the dramatic potential for the tragedy of an extraordinary black noble man, a general. In fact, Shakespeare's source for *Othello*, we are told, was a novella by Giraldi Cinthio. The main thrust of Cinthio's story is this: "Disdemona" met her unhappy fate in choosing to marry a "Moor," a man who is unsuitable for her in every way because of their differences in upbringing (race, religion and education).[18] The black existence and the plot the novella narrates are hardly credible, but the tale raised dramatic possibilities in the creative psyche of an avid and precocious reader/playwright of seventeenth-century England, already noted for his compelling imagination and inventiveness among his audience.

The distant and exotic locale of the tale increases the mythic quality of the story, and could be used to distance the English audience from its cultural bias into accepting a noble black as a central character, especially since the part will be played by a well-known white actor. At any rate, something could be said for a black general whose cultural background lends itself to exotic, adventurous imagination to be supported by the character himself, who, though does not pretend to be a white man, has acculturated himself enough to be taken as one—under certain circumstances.[19] In this regard, the dramatic ploy would be Othello's capacity to think and reason as a general, and as a Christian—which would remove likely thoughts of paganism, or the barbarism that Cinthio's tale implies. With the honor and respect paid to military craftsmanship, Othello could be accepted as deserving the equal status of citizenship—not unknown in Greco-Roman world where slaves, after all, became highly honored citizens. More telling, though, is whether the people in his immediate environment accept him as such, and whether he as a black man is honestly comfortable in such a status.[20] Although the playwright's dramatic questing will not allow him to follow his source closely, there are ideas in the source that obviously strike Shakespeare's psyche, triggering his departure—such as the themes of love, jealousy and revenge. For instance, Shakespeare dramatically refines the love between Othello and Desdemona from the suggestion of corruption that Cinthio gives it, making Iago (albeit through false claims) desire Desdemona, so that Iago uses the fabricated rejection to fuel his passion for revenge. These themes, given the mythic/sentimental quality of the tale, must be focused within dramatic, realistically acceptable but tragic circumstances. But, referring to Cinthio's story as mythic is really consistent with the author who calls fiction "the mythology of the modern world, more in touch with the values and interests of a contemporary audience than the old Greek myths."[21] We can assume he implies that fiction, whether fact-based or not, is a mythic narrative by the nature of its being fictive.

Thus, the realistic/tragic drama of Othello, evolving from the idea-note that struck in the playwright's psyche, through a mythic/secular source, concerns the fate of Othello, a black man, marrying Desdemona, a white woman, and the tragic action generated by that fate. One way for the playwright to cause the tragic consequences to erupt is to test the validity of the love that fashioned the marriage, and the people's acceptance of Othello's nobility and leadership. Apart from the fact of his descent ("I fetch my life and being/

From men of royal siege"[22]), his war accomplishments, which have earned him the generosity of the state of Venice, and license (privileges), have great potential for nobility. But eloping with a daughter of a senator may be one privilege too many, a license that dangerously calls attention not only to Othello as an alien, but also to his blackness. How might these tension-laden factors explode from the idea-kernel?

Obviously, Shakespeare's source gives him the lead—Cinthio's Ensign needs to be engaged more dramatically. The crudity of the source is turned to advantage, imaging Iago, the emotionless, unscrupulous ensign who plays mind-tricks on innocence. The expression gradually achieves its power through the multiplicity of characters that emerge to serve Iago's purpose (Brabantio, Roderigo, Emilia, Cassio and, principally, Desdemona) in destroying Othello's credibility and nobility. These characters, most of whose identities remain hidden or nameless in Cinthio's tale, become dramatic vehicles of Shakespeare's evolving script—puppets under the manipulative, evil-genius fingers of Iago, the catalyst of Othello's objective action.

Shakespeare's Othello, as with most of his plays, developed from mythic-narrative sources, which prompted the idea-note that struck his psyche, storehouse of experiences both factual and imagined. His inventive skills and sense of the dramatic then engaged the idea-note, which has already absorbed his source, to express his drama. However, skills do not automatically guarantee success. The creative process is demanding, and the need to express the idea-note successfully, that is, by finishing the play, racks the playwright's ritual sensibilities, almost robbing the playwright of the ability or confidence to create. It is a fateful questing full of fatal apprehensions of possible failure, either in terms of not completing the play, or of the audience not accepting it. For the playwright's task is to make the mythic fate of his or her central character realistic (that is, like real), in such a way that it engages and becomes acceptable to the audience, at least some audience. It is only by ritual struggle, by a continual summoning of the combative will (the gradual mastering of the idea-note) that the playwright is able to overcome his or her fears and able to express. Regarding the audience acceptance of it, the playwright should understand he or she really has no control, but can only hope.

Cinthio's readers, including Shakespeare (who also might have read it in translation) probably accepted his tale as mythic-fictive, as he intended it— the "mythology of the modern world." Shakespeare takes it and gives it a dramatic form. For that fiction to be engaging as a play to Shakespeare's audience, or to theater audiences in general, particularly because it is presented live, it must have a semblance of reality—in other words, it must be mythic-realistic. Rather than making a straightforward moralistic statement about the unhappiness that results when persons of different races (also of different class, education and religion) marry, Shakespeare, with an imaginative dramatic scope, makes jealousy—that green-eyed monster, which doth mock/ The meat it feeds on"—the ritual ingredient of the idea-note that struck him. Thus, in the adroit hands of Iago (really Shakespeare's), jealousy propels the otherwise magnanimous fate of Othello to catastrophe. Consequently, while nobility and reputation are at stake, and white innocence is shattered by black savagery, the extremes of white hate that schemes and channels that savagery is hardly forgotten. Perhaps Shakespeare intends to make his audience be more critical of its prejudices. If so, that awareness also makes the audience accept the tragic fate of a black hero who falls from grace through the all-too-human flaw of misplaced trust.

The mythic creative processes of the last three playwrights to be examined in this chapter conceive one-act plays: the *Zoo Story* of Edward Albee,[23] *Dutchman* of LeRoi Jones (Amiri Baraka),[24] and *Fool for Love* by Sam Shepard.[25] The process of the first two, for reasons that will be obvious, contrasts each other. A discussion of each playwright's dramatic response to the idea-note that struck the psyche will serve as an initial thrust to a fuller discussion of the plays' structure later in the book.

We know more about the objectives of modern playwrights than about those of the past, through documented interviews, or justification of these objectives in prefaces to their plays. Even so, these must not be taken at face value, for much of what they say about their plays is often after the fact. Of course, there is no reason to doubt what a playwright says about his or her particular play (and sometimes the expression falls short of the intention), but often the intention at the beginning has gone through a series of modifications in the developmental process, which includes readings and workshops. Most playwrights are not fully confident about what they have expressed; some depend on the director and actors to clarify their intentions for them, and others seek the approval of the audience and critics before they could vent their opinions about the work and its objective.

Zoo Story and *Dutchman* were written in about the same period—in the turbulent 1960s. As such, each play can be regarded as a playwright's response to the events of the time. As some critics have noted, one would seem, structurally at any rate, to be a black playwright's inspired reaction or response to the other, a white expression of an American crisis.[26] Although the argument can be supported by the fact that LeRoi Jones was a student in a playwriting workshop of Edward Albee, it is also a fact that the concerns of both playwrights are individually real, and therefore each play can legitimately stand on its own. *Zoo Story* dramatizes the fate of a desperate white individual who finds himself isolated, unable to make connections, living a rather difficult and superficial existence in New York—and this can represent any large American city. *Dutchman* on the other hand dramatizes the fate of an eager black individual in the same city, trying to assimilate in a rather racist culture. Therefore, the source of the idea that struck each playwright's psyche can be said to be factual.

On second thoughts, beyond the factual source, the playwrights seem to be dealing with modern myths of a society, a society that isolates in the case of Albee, and one that makes a black man wish to isolate himself in the case of LeRoi Jones, or Amiri Baraka as he is later known. Each playwright, using his creative imagination, wishes to dissect each particular myth and, by so doing, demythologize it. This seems to be the intention of most absurdist playwrights, as we have gradually come to understand it in their writing, and this makes the expression of both playwrights realize an absurdist vision. This also alters slightly our perception of the source, which can now be qualified as mythic/factual. The factual is especially evident in American playwriting, which often tends to be autobiographical. How then does one come to terms with the absurdist expressions realized by these autobiographical playwrights?

As established, a play, like all creative arts, by the fact of its imaginative expression and individual point of view, and with it being an illusion of reality, is fictive. Hence each play describes its own realism. If what the absurdist playwrights in general are trying to do, with their drama of the undramatic (as their expression has been identified),[27] is to deconstruct that illusion of reality, in order to construct the realities of the human condition, we may indeed pose the question: Does their mode of expression therefore make their drama less fictive, and more real? Perhaps not, since their art is still a subjective and imagined point of view, an art which, in destroying a myth, creates another. However, perhaps their expression makes us perceive more intensely the apparent human condition in the real world. Hence, perhaps we can say their art is intensely realistic—a fictive/surreal? Let us pursue this with *Zoo Story* and *Dutchman* by focusing on the playwrights' probable intentions for the fate of their respective central character.

Albee, in his majority white world, is relating to the factual breakdown of American culture and family, whose individuals are isolated from one another by the mythic, superficial structure of values posed by the system. It is not difficult to understand why Albee's creative instinct is taken by this crisis, committed to expose its mythic foundations. According to interviews and studies on him, he himself has experienced loneliness—from childhood, through high school and to beginning of his career. The creative objective he struggles with as a playwright is to ritualize this isolation, this adversity, so as to shake his audience to a wake-up call, literally from dreamland to the world of naked truth—such that describes the realities of the rampant suicides especially in New York at the time he wrote his play. In this play, Jerry makes a suicidal statement to seemingly complacent Peter, forcing Peter to understand what it means to be isolated. Albee's struggle, to realize his objective through Jerry, aligns his own fate as a lonely man with that of his central character. Let us pursue this alignment of fates.

Although Jerry would seem to reflect the playwright's isolation, he is not the playwright but an agent of him, whose absurdist state of mind needs to ritualize a surreal presence of isolation—or whose idea-note that struck is in need of a fictive/surreal expression. On the surface there is something odd but real about Jerry, who comes to the park to invade and harass the privacy of another individual. As it becomes clearer, it is part of the ritual strategy of the character and the playwright's, to shake up Peter's self-complacency into an awareness of Jerry's isolation. More important, the shake-up must make Peter be aware of his own isolation and, by extension, others who, like the playwright, find themselves in similarly bind. What begins as a mental confrontation (Jerry's intellectual invasion of Peter's isolation), becomes a visually incisive calculation (Jerry's dog story about disconnection), which then compels a physical and taunting manipulation (Jerry's provocation of Peter to defend his claims to the bench with a knife), a final desperate effort to jab Peter's seemingly numb sensibilities into active perception—by extension, the sensibilities of the audience.

The intensification of the strategic confrontation (and Peter really has no breathing space) not only describes Jerry's desperation but also expresses the surreal. In this regard, we may surmise that every strategy Jerry adopts is an intensified condensation of the playwright's related experience, so that Jerry's ritual struggle is also the playwright's. Both are bound by a common fate of shattering the superficial and focus-distorting mirror of status in which Peter (and others like him) obliquely perceives himself and Jerry. The playwright's hope is that the audience also perceives this, otherwise his intention with Jerry is not realized.

In *Dutchman*, LeRoi Jones' psyche was struck by his experiences as a minority black man in majority white America, experiences that reflect the difficulties of survival in a world that is founded on the mythic identities of a black person, and therefore revels in racism. In that world, an attempt to assimilate under such mythic cultural imperatives is an illusion that the playwright wishes to shatter. This mythic conditioning through assimilation enables the surreal vision of the playwright.

As in *Zoo Story*, the fate-action of the central character, in this instance, Clay—who is only too eager to assimilate—indirectly aligns with that of the playwright.[28] We know that LeRoi Jones, like many African-Americans, has tried to assimilate one way or another, all to no avail—that is, in terms of being accepted on equal footing as a black man. It is an attitude of hopelessness that Jones brings to bear on the expression of the idea that struck and on the objective of his central character to assimilate by any means necessary. The playwright evokes the surreal mausoleum of society, "In the flying underbelly of the city"[29] in which the "Dutchman" (mythical in one sense and realistic in another) is both the conveying vessel of plague and slavery, and the communicant vehicle for self-destruct assimilationists like Clay.[30] Encountering Lula, a sexual object or symbol of his assimilation, Clay eagerly warms up to her graphic innuendos, and, even in the face of her pointedly racist attacks, allows himself to be mentally seduced. Clay's fateful/fatal objective is to gratify the sexual propositions being flaunted at him regardless of the racial slurs mixed with the flaunting. He does not defend his rights as a black man until pushed to the wall by Lula's sexual and racist exhibitionism, when it is too late. For Lula counters his apparently violent defense by stabbing him to death.

But perhaps Lula's act of murder has been her plan all along, awaiting a welcome boost at the right time. That idea would seem to coincide with the playwright's surrealist intention, to shock the black audience into becoming aware of its assimilationist inclinations to avoid Clay's fate of death. This suggestion, only implied in the play, is very clear in the author's short essay, "The Revolutionary Theatre:"

> "The Revolutionary Theatre must EXPOSE! Show up the insides of these humans, look into black skulls . . . It must Accuse and Attack because it is a theatre of Victims . . . Clay in *Dutchman*, Ray in *The Toilet*, Walker in *The Slave* are all victims.
>
> In the Western sense they could be heroes. But the Revolutionary Theatre, even if it is Western, must be anti-Western" [31]

Jones' creative process in *Dutchman* resorts to a fictive/surreal mode to impose his point of view on the racial turbulence and civil rights protests of the 1960s. The resulting expression indicts a racist system and, more important, insists that the black individual not compromise his or her black sensibilities for seductive and corruptive white ones. Clay's fate-action probably represents that once taken by playwright. However, it lacks the gained experience of LeRoi Jones, whose fateful/fatal struggle as a black man went from being peaceful and accommodating to being a separatist and a proponent of violent revolutionary action for unqualified liberation from slavery and racism. Jones would go on to express his separatist position more clearly in a subsequent play, *The Slave*.[32] The central character in that play, Walker Wessels, describes the playwright's rather difficult struggle to come to terms with renouncing, and cutting ties with a culture that has promoted such insidious and taunting slave-bind.

Because of the historical conditioning of the blacks in the U.S , the idea-note that struck the creative psyche of most African American dramatists inevitably resonates similar experiences of survival. However, the mode of expression has been different, depending on the various interacting fates that describe that conditioning, and which align with the psychic constitution (stored up experiences) of the playwright, inducing the idea-note that strikes. As such, expressions of the idea-note have varied, from the direct militancy of LeRoi Jones (*The Slave*), through the humanistic tendencies of Lorraine Hansberry (*A Raisin in the Sun*) and the indirect accommodation and celebration of identity of August Wilson (*Joe Turner's Come and Gone*), to the inverted satire of Douglas Turner Ward (*Day of Absence*) or Suzan-Lori Parks (*The America Play*).

Sam Shepard's absurdist creative process, in plays such as *A Fool for Love*, wrestles in a different way with the fate of the individual within the American ideals of societal and family values, values that seem to be male-dominant, and which Shepard ultimately exposes as flawed. This is a struggle for Shepard who had himself striven to bond with his father's and the American ideal.

Within this context is focused the intimacy and the fate of the two principal characters in *A Fool for Love*, Eddie and May[33]. It is difficult to designate the central character in this play because both characters are afflicted by the same fateful/fatal condition—a pursuit of a love that is ideal, but illegitimate because it is incestuous. It is a love that constantly pulls them together and apart. But Eddie seems a better choice as central character; he is the one that always seeks out May to try to rekindle the relationship, though May encourages it by leaving tracks. And though both evoke and are beset by the image of their father, Eddie seems to be the one more focused on and compelled by the image and male bonding. Eddie is the one fascinated by the ideal, which he tries to define his own way, a definition which his father implies is unrealistic compared to his own:

THE OLD MAN: Take a look at that picture on the wall over there. (*he points at wall stage-right. There is no picture but* EDDIE *stares at the wall*) Ya' see that?. . .

EDDIE: (*staring at wall*) Yeah

THE OLD MAN: Ya' know who that is?

EDDIE: I'm not sure.

THE OLD MAN: Barbara Mandrell. That's who that is . . . You heard a' her?

EDDIE: Sure.

THE OLD MAN: Well, would you believe me if I told ya' I was married to her?

EDDIE: (*pause*) No.

THE OLD MAN: Well, see, now that's the difference right there. That's realism.
I am actually married to Barbara Mandrell in my mind.[34]

The "realism" of the father's relationship is a dream of the mind as opposed to that of Eddie's relationship with May—a forbidden reality. It is a difference between theater and real life. However, Shepard, in The Old Man's narrative of a journey in the past (with the old man, May and May's mother) evokes images that not only give the play its wider societal scope, but implicate the American ideal, with words such as "Plymouth" (The Old Man's car), which "Had a white plastic hood ornament on it. Replica of the *Mayflower* I think it was".[35] Ultimately the fate of Eddie, not unlike the playwright's, is the fate of every individual whose fascination with an ideal is flawed by an incestuous (that is, obsessive) involvement of it.

The father's distinction of realism offers an interesting perspective to our construct. Shepard's source is factual/mythic, which strikes an absurdist idea-note in the playwright's psyche, and is expressed as a mythic/surreal. This mode of expression seems to be consistent with the father's objective perception of an American ideal, contrasting Eddie's subjective perception of it—an obsession that insists the ideal is reality. Here, in fact, realism itself is in question. For it is sometimes difficult to determine what is real, and what is an illusion of real. A ready example of this can be made with the fact of the art of television (a medium of the mythic/fictive) and its influences on societal imperatives and values (acquired or imposed means of the factual/realistic). For instance, the superficial and lavish way of living suggested by television drama, or an ad, often misleads the public to emulate it. The analogy almost parallels the delusions of a playwright who insists that his or her play expresses reality, when in fact that reality is only a perception, a realism, of the mind. Shepard often struggles with both concepts (realism and reality) in his plays. In *A Fool for Love*, doors are made to slam with a boom, a reality-action that shocks the audience into a fact of watching a play, an illusion of reality; and narratives, such as the father's, evoke mysterious images of a past that was both real and deceptive. The presence of the father is also an illusory presence of a past reality. These contrasting layers of the seeming real and the illusory define the surreal expression of the play.

These plays will later be put in better perspective in terms of structure. Their discussion here is an attempt to demonstrate the initial thrust of creativity from the idea-note that strikes the playwright's psyche—the beginning of the ritual/creative process that involves the fate of the central character as well as of the playwright. However, the fate of the central character, evolving from the psyche of the playwright, and the subsequent action it describes in the playwright's expression, only partially implicate the fate or life process of the writer. For the expression, and therefore the fate of the central character, is only a response to a particular concern or crisis in the fate process of the playwright, within or outside of himself or herself. It is a crisis or concern to which the writer is committed to give a dramatic expression, without which the playwright cannot find relief. It is a ritual commitment that is often mirrored by the playwright's central characters—Oedipus, Othello, Gogo and Didi, Jerry, Eddie or May, Clay—that is, the objective-action they describe. With these realistic, imagined characters (really figures from the *illud tempus*, the ritual arena in the playwright's psyche), the playwright expresses the concern, realistically, for his or her community. The expression is the message the playwright hopes would become clear and be well received—that is, when the fictional presence of the characters incarnates into real (present) actor-personages in the theater, the community space of live performance. This procedure in itself raises complex issues of realism and reality.

The ritual objective of the playwright, represented by his or her characters, comes at a cost. For all creation demands a struggle, which amounts to the characters' sacrifice as well as the playwright's—their relative commitment to their respective objective in the face of odds. But the crucial implications of the commitment must be understood; in fact, it can only be understood in ritual terms, which can now be restated more clearly.

The playwright broaches the ritual arena or space of his or her psyche in quest of an idea that could generate an expression for the resolution of his or her concern, or of the crisis that has arisen in his or her community. Through the ritual racking of the psyche, an idea potent with dramatic possibilities strikes and is imaged. In his or her attempt to evoke or invoke characters and come to terms with a most feasible expression for resolving the concern or crisis, the playwright, in ritual immersion, finds himself or herself alone in the abyss wrestling with the fateful/fatal elements that suggest themselves at every thought. As noted earlier, the abysmal experience is not unlike the sacrificial experiences of primal artist/archetypes (such as the Yoruba Ogun or the Greek Dionysus) into the *illud tempus* or chthonic realm.[36] Like them, the playwright faces possible extinction, certain insanity, or the obliteration of the idea that struck. However, again like Ogun and Dionysus, the playwright's survival depends on a combative will (to create) that he or she constantly summons throughout the process. This will power enables the playwright to decode and master the idea-codes and tones that explode and litter the abyss of uncertainty, like atoms. The ritual power also enables the playwright to activate a commitment that directs the voice or vision necessary to make relevant choices for the playwright's (as well as his or her central character's) rite of passage. In this regard, the playwright's creative struggle is a ritual attempt in his or her physical world to connect with the metaphysical and then reconnect with the physical with supernal vision—possible answers to certain questions that plague the crisis-laden physical world of playwright's community. As implied, all creative artists suffer or undergo this state of being and non-being, and being again. But what makes the playwright's experience particularly difficult and crucial is his or her realism, that is, the peculiar (practical but rather superficial) relationship the playwright has with his or her created characters—figures that must ultimately animate a realistic, dramatic presence for the playwright's expression on stage.

The interpretive, physical realism on stage, expressive of the playwright's written dramatic codes, is really a physical manifestation of ritual efficacy. It is the physical expression of what both the playwright and central character successfully realized. In Soyinka's terms, it is a "triumph over subsumation through the agency of the will," utterant-gains, so to speak, of will and sacrifice.[37] However, this experience should not be confused with the ritual process of the play's performance, realized by the actor through the director, a ritual enactment that becomes aligned with the audience's ritual experience of it through catharsis. Elsewhere I have explained catharsis in terms of a ritual process in which the artist/priest broaches the *illud tempus* or the chthonic realm of the metaphysical audience (the gods) for a need, on behalf of ritual participants, the physical community or theater-audience. Catharsis comes by way of god-sanctioned efficacy, through the ritual-enactment/performance of the priest-actor for the worshiper-audience.[38] Thus, in a way, catharsis is godsend, but the complex process begins with the playwright.

The playwright stands at the primal stage of the performance process as the shaman-priest whose expression anticipates catharsis, realized in coded messages from the *illud-tempus* and transmitted through the actor-interpreter to the audience. At the point of catharsis in the theater, the playwright, the actor and the audience are all at one with expression and being.

NOTES

1. *Anatomy of Criticism*, 104–107.

2. Luigi Pirandello, *Pirandello's Major Plays* (Evanston, Illinois: Northwestern University Press, 1991).

3. Jean-Paul Sartre, *No Exit and Three Other Plays* (New York: Vintage International, 1989).

4. For a detailed explanation, see "Concepts of Fate," in *Archetypes, Imprecators and Victims of Fate*, ch.1.

5. My notion of hubris (as that defiant arrogance that propels the individual to follow an objective action in one directional course, as the only alternative that individual

could take) follows Corrigan's definition: *Theatre and Search of Fix* (New York: Dell Publishing Co., Inc., 1973), 7.

6. *Theatre in Search of a Fix*, 6–10.
7. Martin Esslin, *Theater of the Absurd* (New York: Doubleday, 1969), 32–33.
8. *Waiting of Godot*, 8–9.
9. *Waiting for Godot*, 28–29.
10. *Waiting for Godot*, 57 and 58.
11. *Waiting for Godot*, 7.
12. See Shakespeare's *King Lear* (The Arden Edition) Act 3, sc2. Edited by Kenneth Muir (London Methuen, 1972), 99–105.
13. Orgel, 188.
14. *Othello* (The Arden Edition) edited by M.R. Ridley (London: Methuen, 1958).
15. For an attempt to construct a perception of Shakespeare's representations of blacks in his works, see Imthiaz Habib, *Shakespeare and Race: Postcolonial Praxis in the Early Modern Period* (Lanham, Maryland: University Press of America, 2000).
16. See, P. Ericson, "Representation of Blacks and Blackness in the Renaissance," *Criticism* 35, 4 (1993): 499–527; Katharine George, "The Civilized West Looks at Primitive Africa: 1400–1800," *The Concept of the Primitive*, ed. A Montagu (NY: Free Press, 1968). Also Elliot H. Tokson, *The Popular Image of the Black Man in English Drama: 1550–1688* (Boston: G.K. Hall, 1982).
17. See, Folarin Olawale Shyllon, *Black People in Britain: 1555–1833* (London: Oxford University Press, 1977).
18. For an analysis of the tale compared with Shakespeare's play, see Frank Kermode "Othello, the Moor of Venice," in *The Riverside Shakespeare*, ed. G. Blakemoore Evans, et al (Boston: Houghton Mifflin, 1974), 1198–1202.
19. This notion of the character, and subsequent ones, must be considered as only one interpretation among various in scholarship.
20. Black, in the Renaissance identifies various racial (alien) groups (Moors, Africans, Indians), and signification (sorrow, mourning, disappointed love, etc). See Tokson, 7. On Othello's idea of his blackness, see Elliott Butler-Evans, "Haply, for I Am Black": Othello and the Semiotics of Race and Otherness," *Othello: New Essays by Black Writers*" ed., Mythili Kaul (Washington, DC: Howard University Press, 1997). Also Ruth Cowhig, "Blacks in English Renaissance and the Role of Shakespeare's Othello," *The Black Presence in English Literature*, ed. David Dabydeen (Manchester: Manchester University Press, 1985), 1–25.
21. See *The Riverside Shakespeare*,1198.
22. Ridley, 16.
23. Edward Albee, *The Zoo Story and the Sandbox* (New York: Dramatists Play Service, 1960).
24. LeRoi Jones/Amiri Baraka, *Dutchman and The Slave* (New York: Morrow/Quill, 1964).
25. Sam Shepard, *A Fool for Love and Other Plays* (New York: Bantam Books, 1984).
26. See Allan Lewis, *American Plays and Playwrights of Contemporary Theatre* (New York: Crown Pulishers, 1965), 253–254.

27. For a summary of what constitutes this type of drama, see introduction to Martin Esslin's *Theatre of the Absurd* (New York: Anchor Books, 1969).

28. Lula, who appears to be the aggressor in this play has been suggested as the central character: See Hugh Nelson, "LeRoi Jones' *Dutchman*: A Brief Ride on a Doomed Ship," *Educational Theatre Journal* 20, 1(March 1968): 53–59. While there is no denying that Lula's action technically describes that of a central character, I think making her one is a misreading of the playwright's intentions. See Larry Neal, "The Black Arts Movement," *The Drama Review* 12, 4(Summer 1968): 29–39.

29. *Dutchman*, 3.

30. For various implications of "Dutchman," see "LeRoi Jones' *Dutchman*."

31. "The Revolutionary Theatre," *Home, Social Essays* (New York: William Morrow, 1966), 211.

32. LeRoi Jones/Amiri Baraka, *Dutchman and The Slave.*

33. Sam Shepard, *Fool For Love and Other Plays*.

34. See *Fool for Love*, 27.

35. *Fool for Love*, 32.

36. For comparative parallels of Ogun and Dionysus, see "Introduction" in Wole Soyinka, *The Bacchae of Euripides* (New York: W.W. Norton. 1973), v–xi.

37. "The Fourth Stage," *Myth*, 149.

38. See "Introduction," in *Archetypes*, 7.

Chapter Three

Ritual Impulses and the Playwright: *The Dramatic Structure*

The idea-note thus strikes the Muse-ic of the playwright's expression, potent with the inventive impulses that the playwright will use decode the dramatic contents embedded in the idea, contents that will eventually constitute a play. We shall begin to focus on these impulses, generative liberators, so to speak, that help transform the idea-note and its contents into an expressed dramatic structure with its subject, theme, plot and denouement. We will consider these ritual impulses from the point of view of the central focus or character, who is the ritual vehicle of the idea that strikes, and with whom or which the playwright is able to respond to the dramatic implications of the ritual impulses. For it is the central focus, even if a virtual one at first, that projects the image that arouses the impulses.

It must be understood, the impulses define a two-way relationship between the playwright and the text—they not only incite the playwright, they establish the structure of the text. They not only originate from the playwright as dramatic devices of expression, they impose their structural presence on the expression. Hence, when I talk about the subject, the theme or the action (plot) of a play, I do not refer to literary and analytical devices of literary critics, which often tend to exclude the playwright even if assumed. Rather, I mean the ritual implements that serve the playwright in bringing his expression to form, consciously or otherwise. What the literary or theater critic does in effect, reading or watching a play, is seeking the playwright's vision through these impulses in the text, but the critic's terminologies are mere jargons of the trade—they tend not to reflect the emotional condition that the impulses bring to bear on the playwright. The attempt to describe the impulses in this chapter echoes the objective of the critic, except that it does so from the point of view of the ritual vehicle, the playwright.

Ritual Impulses and the Playwright: The Dramatic Structure

As suggested in the previous chapters, the creative process involves two parallel and similar constructs, the psychically conceived process and the physically expressed one. Ultimately the ritual objective of the psychical becomes manifest in and aligned with the ritual objective of physical, and this results in the gradual expression of the idea. Similarly, the fate of the playwright, initiated by the mental process, becomes aligned with that of the central focus or character of the writer's dramatic expression. While the last chapter tries to concretize the probable dramatic content of the idea, or (in terms of muse-ic) to define the color/tone-loaded possibilities or variables of the note that struck, this chapter focuses on the structural devices of drama that impact that idea-note into a formal, tonal expression.

Indeed, we are dealing with the transition from metaphysical probabilities to physical possibilities, and we can speak of this in terms of birthing. A child being born crosses from an imagined metaphysical environment to a familiar physical one—that is, from the point of view of the living in already existing realities; to the newborn, the process is from a familiar to the unfamiliar. In its physical existence, according to African (particularly Yoruba) perception, the probable fate of the newborn, chosen in the metaphysical world, must align itself with the fate process that infant must begin to describe in the physical world—from birth to adolescence; through adulthood, vocation, and possibly marriage; to old age and finally death, when the soul would return to the metaphysical world. These transitions mark the rites of passage of the child in the living world. Each transition is also like birthing from one stage of existence to another, therefore an important stage of reconnection with that primal stage crossing from the metaphysical to the physical.

The fate process with its stages of transition presupposes a chosen and sanctioned fate in the metaphysical world, and a ritual struggle that describes each transition. Apparently the ritual struggle defines an attempt to recall and follow the course of the fate chosen in the metaphysical world, the exact memory of which begins to fade into oblivion as the newborn enters the physical world. As such, the recall can only manifest through a concentrated effort of ritual immersion of being, hence, the various ritual ceremonies, or the transitional rites, that are brought to bear on being in order to determine the right course of fate.

To illustrate the struggle of ritual immersion, Soyinka describes an artist potential that recalls the fate of an artist-archetype, the Yoruba hero-god Ogun, who led the expedition of gods (the expedition of reunion) through the "primordial marsh," the amorphous jungle that separates the metaphysical world of gods and ancestors from the physical world of humans[1]. It was an annihilating experience that Ogun, principle of creativity, championed and survived through the force of his combative will. It is a struggle that all creative artists experience one way or another.

But perhaps a more pertinent analogy to grasp in terms of our playwriting concept is the one we have so far implied with the creation of the voice, the voice intoned. A voice-note is a physical product of a psychical state of feeling, be it of joy or sadness. However, that single-note creation is loaded with color and meaning to be explored, a meaning and tonal color from the depths of being that translates into an expression. Aligning with the emotional condition of the depths, the note conveys a meaning-ful and focused expression to the listener or, in fact, to the voicer—since it is possible to intone and convey meaning to just oneself. Either way, the expression (ritualized through the struggle of alignment and transition) seeks response, whether from the listener who may empathize with the singer, or from the voicer who may feel some therapeutic relief. But more important is the fact of the metaphysical voice-note, loaded with feeling, an explorable feeling that seeks to be understood by the impact of its expression and, perchance, to draw response. The Tibetan Bhuddist monks understand this metaphysical significance of the voice-note as they intone from the depths of being to make contact with spirituality.

Let us now bring the transitional state of idea-note and expression back to the playwright, the voicer whose voice-note is the raw or root idea that struck or generated, through a ritual confrontation and struggle, from its metaphysical entity. This idea is potent with explorable thoughts and facts that need be communicated through an act of intoning or physical expression before it can be understood. To get a more visual image of the idea-note and its potency, we could, if only for a moment, liken it to kernel whose hard outer covering encases its expressive seed-elements, that is, the playwriting elements of structure—image, situation, subject matter, theme and plot. It is the idea-kernel that the playwright must crack (like as a singer cracks and vibrates a note on the vocal cords) to discover and explore its nutty or problematic structural elements.

These elements of the cracked idea-kernel, when released to be expressed and from the first images they conceive, appear to concern the fate of another individual; in reality though, they concern the fate of the playwright. This need not confuse us, but should further enhance our understanding of what has already been established—the playwright's struggle to align his or her fate with that of the central character, a creation of the playwright. It is the individuality (spirituality) of the playwright that has generated the idea through his or her own experience, physical or mental, without which the particular idea may not have struck. However, the concerns of the playwright that initiated the idea parallel or involve those of other individuals constituting the playwright's community–that is, people for whom the playwright feels he or she is writing. Among these individuals the playwright must choose (consciously or otherwise) a likely and most appropriate person (imagined or known) to help the playwright express the concerns. It is the only way, albeit indirectly, that the playwright can understand not only the concerns, but also himself or herself in relation to the individual he or she chooses. In this regard, there are two options open to the playwright. The idea and its elements may attract other individuals to help the playwright express the concerns, or the playwright may choose to express the idea with only the chosen individual, an individual that is relatively nobody else but the playwright. I shall in due course discuss more fully what I have called a monotonic-monologic expression, but this relationship the playwright has with his or her central character is perhaps more evident in consciously autobiographical expressions.

Suppose then the playwright has chosen to intone or express the idea directly with his or her characteristic voice, or indirectly with another individual or individuals, how does he or she go on to correctly decipher and express an idea born in the amorphous recesses of the psyche? Given the fact that the stated impulses or elements of structure are matters of craft that need not be consciously determined at the initial stage of the creative process, it is easy to think that the idea also happens subconsciously. But the play cannot depend on the subconscious alone to express itself; other conditions prevail.

In reality, the idea that strikes the psyche is part of the stored up information-system in the psyche, information from various experiences of the writer, in the immediate or the outside community. While experience is not necessarily determined by an individual's age, it is a fact of creativity that the more the individual experiences (through observation or reading or direct encounter), the more that individual acquires the knowledge that informs his or her creativity. For the psyche is a storehouse of experiential encounters with various life processes, psychically or physically. And, since a dramatic idea constitutes a set of codes (messages, impulses of structure, characters, etc.), experiences serve as major influence on the playwright in decoding the idea that struck, determining or imaging the possible central character, and using that character to focus the impulses. Eventually the impulses, at least after the first draft of expression, will help in return focusing the expressed drama. Further, experience enables the individual respond to things in a way that demonstrates the individual's knowledge and insight. These insights of experience facilitate the playwright's dramatic impulses.

Anticipating the end product of the playwright's achievement, the playwright must focus the contents of the idea with the central character, with whom the community/audience empathizes, or upon whom that community reacts. For the community is by no means a passive being; it receives and reacts, depending on the message of the *illud tempus* script and its conditions or requirements for the resolution of the crisis at hand in the living world.

Apparently there are two major differences in community response—a subjective/accomodating (empathic) or objective/critical (Epic) response. Each response has its cathartic inducement.

Let us illustrate the fact of experience and of impulses used by the playwright by going back to Sophocles and his creation of *Oedipus Rex*. Sophocles, through a mental fateful/fatal, indeed ritual, consideration of the myth of Oedipus, evokes an idea of the quest of Oedipus, that is, Oedipus' fate of searching for the killer of Lauis, really a search for the truth that would resolve a community crisis. While the idea involves another individual in the name of Oedipus, it is generated by Sophocles' experience of the human world, an experience that reflects his own concern about truth searching (and it might be a particular truth in Sophocles' community), an endeavor that could boomerang on the searcher since truth is relative. That idea, the note that struck or the kernel cracked, is potent with possibilities yet to be physically expressed by Sophocles. Fortunately, this idea derives from a narrative myth-source that Sophocles could draw on—some dramatists are not that fortunate.

According to his myth-source, Oedipus has no other choice but to confront the fate he is running away from. This irony of the human condition must have unleashed Sophocles' sensitive and creative impulses that would help dramatize and structure the action his play—Oedipus' quest for truth. For Sophocles to simply dramatize the existing narrative, the running away of Oedipus that results in killing his father and marrying his mother would not be worth his while, nor his audience's who already knew such a tale. But since we know Sophocles' interests in character, it is possible to speculate what impulses helped wrench or decode from his raw idea-note the tone-colors of his physical expression. These impulses, induced by the myth-source and Sophocles' experience of people and his environment, also must have directed the playwright to focus on the traits of Oedipus, on the intoxicant that willed the character to a desperate committed action, in spite of grave consequences and nature of the action itself. Thus begins in Sophocles' psyche, perhaps through an image of Oedipus gorging his eyes out, the ritual struggle to structure or express drama from raw idea.

For an action such as Oedipus', conditioned by character traits, to be dramatically functional, or for Oedipus' intoxicant to activate itself, it would have to be initiated by a crisis that challenges his characteristic capacities as a truth-seeking individual. Such a crisis is suggested by the final sequences of the myth-source—Oedipus, renowned as a riddle solver, is confronted with another riddle. This riddle, to know the identity (the truth) of the killer of Laius, hopes to resolve the crisis at hand, the plague. The riddle appears at first to be easier than that of the Sphinx, especially if the gods could help with a hint. But there's the rub—the gods and their hints—they can be as clear as they are nebulous. Based on his religious beliefs, Sophocles may once have confronted this ambiguous nature of the gods' pronouncements. In fact, resolving the ambiguity is a common human plight with a potential for a tragic catastrophe. As such, the ambiguity could be posed to confront the character of Oedipus and, as a result, generate the impulses of Sophocles' drama, which ritualizes Oedipus' tragic dilemma and catastrophe.

Oedipus' character traits, in fact, might not be foreign to the creating sensibilities of Sophocles—that is, if we contend the fact that, one way or another, the writing often betrays the writer. Even though the myth-source provides some guide, the empathic affinities of the traits to Sophocles' artistic temperament could have helped suggest, perhaps first the impulsive image (Oedipus gorging his eyes out), then the dramatic situation embedded in the raw idea, an image and a situation that reveal the hubristic impulse, the intoxicant, that leads Oedipus to his demise as a tragic victim. The situation might have been clearly perceived and expressed as follows: A goodly king, who has the welfare of his people at heart and who has already demonstrated his capacities as a riddle-solver (a seeker of truth), puts himself in a bind seeking the cause of the plague afflicting his people, even though the truth may critically involve him. This situation, a physical explanation of the psychical raw-idea that struck, thus fleshed out may lead to finding other dramatic factors and impulses of the cracked kernel.

At this situational point, playwrights differ as to the right strategy to take in searching for those factors, or eliciting those impulses. Some would rather continue to strain their psychical resources to wrestle out, mentally, the action of the play; others prefer to throw themselves unguardedly on the blank page to skirmish, that is, writing randomly until they strike a positive direction. Both brooding strategies are demanding ritual experiences in an effort to realize a dramatic expression.

Sophocles' sensibilities, however, may choose to explore and import other dramatic factors or impulses regarding Oedipus, even before locating the situation. One involves the problematic fact of Oedipus's character, which Sophocles may use to define the subject and theme of his impending play. A perception of these factors perhaps can be explained through an understanding of the world view of traditional cultures such as classical Greece, a world view that affirms the irreducible connection between character and fate. As stated earlier, in some African cultures such a connection is implicit in any action of ritual, the fact that it is character that wills action, which results in whatever fateful/fatal consequences present themselves for the character. In other words, a character describes his or her fate-action with characteristic trait and combative will.

With this in mind, let us pursue Sophocles' possible impulses of subject and theme for his play. His objective, to recreate his myth-source of Oedipus by dramatizing the character traits that lead Oedipus to his catastrophe, should easily fall in line with the fate-idea struck in his psyche, and with the image or the situation that the idea has yielded. In other words, the drama of character that Sophocles contemplates is possible not only within the frame of the irony of fate that catches up with Oedipus, but also within the fate-action that irony describes, an action whose combative will identifies Oedipus' character. That combative will conditions Oedipus' intoxicant, his egotism, which embodies headstrong traits such as impulsiveness, pride, rashness, quickness to temper, etc. It is this fate, this quest, this will, this physical structure of playwriting process that is evoked through the playwright's mental exploration of the idea-note or the cracked kernel, and becomes concretized through physical (writing) skirmishes, so to speak.

This understanding helps us further to describe the stages of the playwright's creative process even more clearly. A physical stimulation (the source that provokes the playwright objective to write a play, for instance, fate-myth of Oedipus) engages a metaphysical questing, a ritual struggle that confronts the variable forces of the *illud tempus* (the racking of the psyche). This ritual sacrificial immersion gives birth to a physical idea-kernel (a potential image), which is the explorable visual and concrete counterpart of the metaphysical entity (the idea-note that struck). When the objective-action of the central character, for instance Oedipus' quest, is conceived by the playwright, through persistent ritual immersion that cracks and explores (dissects, deconstructs, analyzes) the idea-kernel, then the subject and theme of the play can be perceived and subsequently described. However, this may not be possible until the initial expression of the drama is realized.

To reiterate, the subject of a play is what the drama is about; the theme of the play is a concise expression of the play's idea. Often, the theme is mistaken for the subject, by combining subject-opposites (love versus hate, or good and evil), which is a matter of conflict, or by identifying the theme in a word (for instance, a theme of jealousy), which is a matter of subject. While this notion of a theme is possible in literary criticism, it is hardly sufficient for the visual and dramatic impulses of the playwright's creative questing. For it is through defined or expressed perception a playwright can better shape his or her play, and thus provide the visual and dramatic needs that would later serve the director and the actor, and ultimately engage the audience.

Of course, it is possible that the theme at first suggests itself in one word or in word-contrasts; if so, such a word or word-phrase needs fleshing out in visual and dramatic terms. For instance, if the thematic word conceived for *Oedipus Rex* is questing, really a possible subject of the play, that thematic word, or that subject in fact has to do with Oedipus' objective—questing for certain truth (that is, the truth of Lauis' death, which implicates Oedipus' identity). However, to make this thematic word or this subject workable for the playwright, it needs fleshing out, visually and with a dramatic ingredient, in a thematic statement that constitutes the idea of the play. Such a statement would suggest the possible action of Oedipus as well as the consequences motivated by the conflicts of that action. This thematic statement will allow the playwright to see his or her drama in one negotiable stretch, just as the playwright expects the reader or viewer to eventually perceive that statement, although in whatever form the reader or viewer chooses.

I say negotiable because the theme, whether the playwright thinks about it before or after the physical expression of the play, is subject to review or modification. For instance, if Oedipus' conflict has to do with his own fate, that is, the choices his character/will forces him to make, a theme or thematic statement suggested by this fate is dependent on those choices Oedipus makes describing his fate. Let us say the subject of *Oedipus Rex* is "Search for Truth;" its thematic statement, with a consequential (dramatic) ingredient, can be expressed as follows: The search for truth may be so driven by an intoxication of the will, which is blind to reason, that the search eventually destroys the person who searches. Or: The search or quest for truth can so intoxicate a willful person to a point of delirium that he finally destroys himself. Such a thematic statement implicates not only the conflicting egotistic drive of Oedipus, but also the consequence of that drive.

Subject and theme are part and parcel of playwright's impulses to dramatize a particular fate of his or her central character, for instance, Sophocles' impulses and the particular fate of Oedipus in his quest of truth. These impulses develop when the fateful questing of Oedipus, along with its fatal consequential objective-action becomes aligned and harmonized with the fate of Sophocles, that is, his objective-impulse to dramatize Oedipus' quest for truth. It is an objective-impulse that negotiates with the objective of Oedipus to find out the truth about the killer of Laius and, subsequently, the truth of Oedipus' identity. However, there is no need to see the quest for the killer of Laius and the quest for Oedipus' identity as two separate objectives, as some critics tended to imply; in reality, one is a condition of the other and, therefore, both are inextricably bound. [2]

Fate alignment and harmony, between the playwright and his or her central character, results in what I have come to conceive as the "happy idea."[3] This is so because at the moment of harmony the playwright clearly perceives the idea-image that would help carry the central character's objective-action through the playwright's expression. For instance, apart from the suggestion provided by his myth-source, Sophocles might have impulsed the structural progression of Oedipus' quest and action first by coming to terms with a thematic statement, mentally or otherwise. Through such a statement, Oedipus' quest for truth falls in harmony with Sophocles' own dramatic quest—both quests bonded, as it were, to the same fate-process. However, influential to that bonding is a possible "happy idea" relating to Oedipus' objective-action, the idea-image of "fate" that has dogged Oedipus since childhood, which now becomes a dramatic factor in the present time of the play, which the playwright uses to its advantageous effect. It is not the fate devised by Apollo, although it has to do with it; neither is it the fate that describes Oedipus' objective-action—these factors only made the "happy idea" more crucial as a dramatic device. Rather, it is the fate that prompts Oedipus not to be limited in his questing by reasons provided by others—reasons implied by Apollo's prediction that torment his heart, reasons that slap him in the face through Teiresias' revelation, Jocasta's slight on prophets and finally the ironic disclosure of the Messenger from Corinth. It is the fate that binds Oedipus to his own oath and curse, the intoxicant that compels his impulsive reasoning even at the cost of possible destruction, a self-inflicted fate that indicts him and from which he seeks to exonerate himself. These (elements of subject and theme) are the ritual impulses that commit the playwright to the development of his or her play, what projects a successful dramatization of both the quest of playwright and central character.

Although "happy idea" has to do with the fate of the central character, it is not fate itself as it seems to be in *Oedipus*. In *Othello*, the fate of Othello is propelled by the handkerchief, the image-idea that Shakespeare uses as a dramatic factor to its fullest consequential advantage. We can say that at the elation-heightened point in which Shakespeare's "fate" aligns with his central character's, the playwright sees the crucial possibility of the handkerchief realizing Othello's fate-process, whose egotistic traits are, perhaps, not unlike those of Oedipus'. What begins as a simple practical implement (Othello's wedding gift to Desdemona), becomes entangled with, and is dangerously supported by Othello's fate (the superstitions that Othello provides the handkerchief become critical to his marriage with Desdemona), so that Iago easily uses the implement to destroy the marriage and Othello. On second thoughts, the oath and curse (image of fate) proclaimed by Oedipus is similar to the handkerchief presented and empowered by Othello, both are ritual devices that come full circle to haunt and destroy their respective central character.

The playwright can begin a physical rendering of his play, with some knowledge of his or her subject, theme or situation, or as soon as the playwright images the objective of his or her central character . However, the playwright may choose to continue the ritual rigors of mental construction, with the hope of conceiving a plot structure for the proposed play. Let us continue to use the familiar *Oedipus Rex* as an example, to suggest how Sophocles (through such ritual engagement) probably devised the plot of his play. It should be noted that we are dealing with an already written play, whose plot structure can easily be determined. The planning would not be that easy for a play being freshly developed; ritual rigors of plot making could be very demanding. Should the playwright proceed to engage the impulses of plot making, it is advisable that he or she outlines a tentative structure based on what he or she has imaged for the central character—this will be revised and fine-tuned later after the initial draft of the physical expression. Some playwrights, like the present author, would rather let that structure develop intuitively as they write, relying on their creative power to instruct them. The product of such a procedure is also subject to revision.

Suppose then Sophocles decided to go on to respond to impulses of the plot structure for *Oedipus Rex*. Through the impulses that made him perceive or define subject and theme, Sophocles has realized the objective of Oedipus—the search for the truth, which would implicate Oedipus' identity. Because Oedipus is a hothead compelled by his egotistic propensity, Sophocles already sees Oedipus' commitment to that search for truth in place—for the hotheadedness will make Oedipus pit himself against all oppositions or conflicts to his objective.

In addition, Sophocles realizes personal stakes for Oedipus (suggested by the myth-source), stakes that would make Oedipus' commitment intoxicative. The reason for his wearing the crown in Thebes had to do with a riddle he solved during his flight from Corinth, the riddle of the Sphinx. That riddle, and the present one concerning the death of Laius, are so crucially similar, in terms of their demand for Oedipus' reputation as a riddle solver to validate itself. The present, not unlike the situation in the past, anticipates the much-desired efficacy of relief from a death-dealing crisis, and therefore a continued divine faith in Oedipus. Sophocles might have perceived, sensed, or come to terms with the intense structural graph that the play describes, situational incidents in which Oedipus finds himself dangling as if on a tightrope, fighting for his life against all oppositions to his success and survival—or so it seems. As Sophocles eventually would focus it, Oedipus' conviction to pursue the truth is, ironically and tragically, driven by the intoxicant in his character.

Sophocles' creative psyche is, therefore, confronted with fateful/fatal possibilities, the intensive demands of tragic heroism, in which Oedipus is his own ritual conflict. But for Sophocles to physically commit himself to writing, if he has not done so already, he may need to conceive a skeletal outline of an action for Oedipus, for or against which the objectives of other characters would logically fall in place. Such a skeleton may be stated as follows: First, Oedipus with his heroic stature puts a curse on everybody, including himself, should they know the killer of Laius but fail to expose him. It must be noted that a curse is ritual implement of fate that seeks justice through the efficacy of a punishment, an action that is judgmentally levied. By so doing, Oedipus launches a critically binding circumstance, one that demands an intense and irrevocable commitment to root out the criminal. Thus, it would seem Oedipus has ironically set himself on the dangerous tightrope.

This initial intense thrust, through obstacles that confront Oedipus' intoxicant, leads to the second level of the structural graph. Certain incidents (suggested by the myth-source but recreated in Sophocles' alert creative psyche) arise to activate this second stage—the pronouncement that the seer, Teiresias, makes, the explanations of fate (undependability of prophecies) that Oedipus' wife, Jocasta, tries to give; and the revelations of identity that a messenger from Corinth makes, regarding Oedipus' supposed parents in Corinth. These incidents triggered by the source impact Oedipus' critical situation, allowing the playwright to align himself with the experience that constitutes the second stage of Oedipus' objective-action. Thus, racked by the incessant prodding of doubt and self-examination, Oedipus is compelled to send for the Shepherd, the only one that knows the truth about his identity, even though Oedipus does so at the expense of possible consequent disaster. At any rate, the decision he takes seems inevitable, since it is the only direction on the tightrope that Oedipus (character and all) has set himself. He must strive on the best he could, forward and honorably, to avoid losing his balance and falling midway. The point of return has been ignored and long gone. The question that arises is whether fighting for honor to the end ultimately bodes any efficacious good. Simply put, will Oedipus realize the truth he seeks? And if so, what then? That question has been raised since Sophocles sets the focus in terms of Oedipus' objective; now the question comes to a head, demanding immediate answer. Again, it is possible to argue that Sophocles in reality had the source to go by, that the objective and consequence are well described by his myth-source, and therefore the question seems irrelevant. But again we must remember that the way Sophocles scripted these impulses of action was a dramatic choice he had to struggle with.

In directing, the crucial question is often referred to as the Major Dramatic Question (MDQ). The answer that the central character seeks, which is a matter of the climax, could be fuzzy to the playwright for a long time; in fact, the playwright may not know the answer until it happened, informing what comes after as a resolution, that is, the final part of the plot. Should the playwright have an idea of the answer, it should remain tentative and changeable, otherwise the expression of the play might turn out contrived. Sophocles' advantage of the myth-narrative is explored to the last detail with dramatic efficiency. He pitches Oedipus' ironic realization of the recklessness of his pursuit as a fitting and logical climax of the plot, one that compels a comparable reaction from the central character—the gorging out of his eyes—and resolves the playwright's objective of giving dramatic expression to the idea-note that struck his psyche. Elsewhere we shall relate to the climax; for now, suffice to know that it is the answer to the central character's objective and provides a resolution, the final stage of the central character's fate-action. It is an impulse that Sophocles has conceived through the dramatic development of Oedipus' action.

It must be stressed that a playwright does not have to define a plot outline before he or she begins writing a play. As stated, some playwrights use the first draft to explore possibilities, during which the ritual impulses intuitively, albeit randomly, feed into the playwright's expression. At the end of the exploratory process, the playwright should have a clearer perception of what he or she wishes to dramatize, and the impulses become more consciously conceived.

Let us consider *Waiting for Godot*. In terms of our creative concept, the differences between the action-dramatic *Oedipus Rex* and the idea-dramatic *Waiting for Godot* are marked by the each playwright's reaction to the ritual impulses. In an action-dramatic, the playwright channels the impulses towards focusing a major objective-action for the central character, an action whose commitment (through conflict and stakes) raise an element of consequentiality. In an idea-dramatic, the playwright imports the impulses to develop an intellectual argument proposed by the playwright through a central character or focus. Although an objective-action exists in this type of play, it is de-emphasized to project the thought-provoking argument of the playwright.

Other apparent differences apply. In *Oedipus* dialogue is often formally consecutive and sequential, whereas in *Waiting*, it is realistically cryptic, and non sequitur. In terms of cosmology, as we have seen, both plays were religiously motivated, one by the classical Greek belief system, the other by the questioning of, and ambiguity in the established Catholic or Christian faith, indeed, in the fate of mankind. While Sophocles accepts his religious bias and takes it for granted, Beckett is critical and questioning, using his skepticism to develop an intellectual discourse. These factors naturally come into play when the idea-note strikes and is transformed into expression through ritual impulses that impose themselves on the idea-note.

As established, the physical thought that provoked Beckett's idea-note for *Godot* was Saint Augustine's philosophical explication on salvation, which asks the believer to hope as well as despair. This thought, which has often been in the playwright's mind, resurfaces in his constantly probing creative psyche. We can determine the absurd nature of the probing by what we know of Beckett as a writer whose experiences (in tune with our modern circumstances) has been conditioned by the absurdity of life's fateful/fatal processes, in a world that has been devastated by human strife in various wars, experiences that seemed, to Beckett, in conflict with and a paradox to the Christian vaunted explanation of God's design for humankind. Saint Augustine also might have raised such a contradiction that afflicted his own tumultuous world; but his rigidly disciplined Christian attitude and ascetic existence must have prevailed to propose a palliative. Not so Beckett's atheistic attitude, which stood up to the challenge of creative investigation. For Saint Augutine's non-committal statement is designed to throw the question back at the inquirer, forcing him or her consider the situation of Christ on the cross flanked on both sides by two thieves seeking salvation in the metaphysical world.

In Beckett's absurd world, Saint Augustine's statement assumes its most critical and paradoxical impulse, which the playwright engages with a pessimistic ritual struggle in order to express it dramatically. The thematic impulse (the intellectual idea or argument) that strikes him for the physical execution of his play may be expressed thus: Salvation for humankind has a fifty-fifty-chance of expectation[4]. Since the playwright wishes to focus on this idea more than the action that generates from it, he explores ways to engage and stimulate his audience with the argument both intellectually and visually.

The thematic impulse, conceived when the idea-note strikes, may be enough to initiate the characters of a play, and therefore induce the playwright to physicalize his or her play. When such characters appear, it may be wise to image them in a situation and therefore probe their authenticity and characteristics, and subsequently use them to enable the play. Vladimir and Estragon (Gogo and Didi) may have evolved with such probing. The image projected may be that of two tramps waiting for somebody that does not appear. Through such an image, their individual characteristics gradually became consistent with the playwright's absurdist idea of salvation.

Both characters, buffeted by circumstances of modern existence, are plausible candidates for Augustine's religious paradox, and Beckett's absurdist vision of the human condition, facilitating conflicting ideologies and contradictory religious intellectualism. Both have similar states of existence as tramps; both seem to be supportive of each other, without which support existence is unbearable; both are not unlike the biblical two thieves of Augustine's analogy. However, they both describe diametrically different characteristics and disagree on issues, which make one intolerant and pessimistic about any idea of survival, and the other more accommodating and optimistic, with a tolerant philosophical view of life. The dramatic question is, who of these characters has more chance of salvation?

If the characters have not motivated Beckett enough to begin writing his play, the question of salvation would seem to put a plot-outline in place. First is the fact that the two tramps are waiting for some salvation, their objective-action. They seem to have some idea of this salvation that a character called Godot psychically evokes for them, a personality they hope would gratify them with his physical presence. However, their waiting compels them to do things to bide the time to counteract the boredom of waiting. The clownish physical activities they invent, through the playwright's ritual impulse, not only allow Beckett to express the characters' rather comical endeavor, but also the more important thematic, intellectual discourse on salvation. Sometimes inventing these activities is difficult, which often makes the characters desperate and in despair of their inability to come up with new ideas or any idea at all.

In the process of waiting and the playwright's ritual immersion, two other characters evolve—Pozzo and Lucky. These characters in a way replicate the first two, in terms of their isolation, complementary characteristics and, of course, salvation—although they are not physically looking for salvation, they are in need of it by their isolated and strained dependency as master and servant. The replication serves Beckett well. It has a cumulative effect that intensifies the playwright's intellectual discourse on the fifty-fifty chanciness of salvation. At any rate, regarding Gogo and Didi's waiting, Pozzo and Lucky become objects of their clownish activities. At first, the tramps mistake one of the intruders for the person for which they were waiting; then, because of the puzzle Pozzo and Lucky create for Gogo and Didi, the tramps sound the intruders at every turn, playing them off like victims of their boredom of waiting.

All the tramps' clowning and syncopated antics-repartee are rituals of the physical action that the playwright's impulses evoke, to engage the audience visually. Intangible as they may seem, they are a necessary physical complement to Beckett's intellectual thematic discourse on salvation as a chancy expectation. Furthermore, Pozzo and Lucky's arrival implicate the chanciness—the seemingly hopeless and delicate relationship that exists between the two highlights that existing between Gogo and Didi. However, if Beckett means to emphasize salvation as an objective-idea for his expression, he would have to engage his audience further than that. In other words, his creative impulses must seek to evoke and ritualize dramatic pointers that would establish his thematic discourse.

As stated in the previous chapter, Beckett attempts to define this thematic graph in three instances. First is his use of the biblical source, the story of the two thieves, which suggestively parallels the situation of the two tramps.[5] As the initial impetus to Beckett's thematic graph, it poses the thematic question, which of the two, if any at all, could be saved like one of the two thieves? When Pozzo and Lucky enter, that question deepens as the doubt of salvation escalates. Pozzo and Lucky's survival of the frustrations of hoping is, like Gogo and Didi's, very much dependent on either of them, although Pozzo is the master and Lucky the servant or underdog. For Pozzo's hope, to sell Lucky at the market (a slave-market ?), placed against his dependency on Lucky, is doubtful. The circumstance does not make the idea of salvation positive for either of them, nor for Gogo and Didi for the matter.

Lucky's monologue marks the second and center stage of Beckett's thematic discourse.[6] Beckett finds in Lucky a useful and significant agency for the verbal expression of his thematic discourse—Lucky, whose status is obviously worse than Gogo and Didi since he is a slave, is an anathema to freedom. Perhaps the only thing he has control over is his creative gift, of dance and philosophical discourse, which he is capable of turning on when he wishes, even at the risk of being whipped. For he can be very stubborn, and it is only after severe threats from his master that he gives expression to his creativity. To compound the significance of Lucky's creative gift, Pozzo's own intellectuality is dependent on it. And perhaps this is the reason why Lucky gives in at all, knowing Pozzo's dependency satisfies his own dependency on his master's hard-earned generosity for sustenance, in whatever meagre form the sustenance comes. But more important (and Pozzo knows this but will not admit it), Lucky's expression has the therapeutic, ritual power (the muse-ic) that sustains Pozzo's survival—a need that often shows up Pozzo's threats as bullying tactics of a paranoia. This attitude and relationship between master and slave is somewhat familiar—it may recall the psychological foundations of paternalistic system in American slavery. Ultimately, both Pozzo and the plantation master seem more dependent on Lucky and the slave than the other way round, making salvation all the more hopeless in achievement. In *Godot*, this circumstance is more apparent the second time Pozzo and Lucky come around when Pozzo has become blind and Lucky dumb.

Lucky's diatribe is an expression of the ritual impulses of his creative process. It is, in fact, a physical example of the profusion of images that rack the creative psyche when the creative artist, for example the playwright, broaches and quests the metaphysical arena, a ritual struggle that conceives and concretizes the abstract idea in the psyche. Like a Muse, an inspiration, an inciting agent, a note, or an abstract thought, Lucky's hat is his fateful/fatal motivating implement of expression. Suffused with creative power, it ritualizes Lucky's discourse on the paradoxical nature of the fate of Man. In some cultural worldview, such as the Yoruba, this physical power symbolizes the physical head and originates from a metaphysical counterpart, which incites its earthly presence to deliberate on its physical existence at a philosophical remove. Lucky's dance is a gestural complement of that discourse and therefore both dance and verbal expression express the same intellectual argument.

Here, at this center stage of the thematic graph, Beckett's creative idea aligns with Lucky's. At first, the monologue seems an impenetrable gibberish, and for the most part it probably is. But the first few lines, as an impetus to the inspired, intoxicated utterance, offer a probable interpretation of the whole:

> Given the existence as uttered forth in the public
> works of Puncher and Wattmann of a personal
> God quaquaquaqua with white beard
> quaquaquaqua outside time without extension
> who from the heights of divine apathia divine
> athambia divine aphasia loves us dearly with
> some exceptions for reasons unknown but time
> will tell . . .[7]

It is a pessimistic thought that puts in doubt the existence of the Christian God, the absolute arbiter for justice and wisdom for the attainment of salvation[8]. It is the psychical conflict of Beckett's creative process, of Lucky's monologue and dance, and of the ritualized dramatic expression. The resolution of this conflict forms the third part of the thematic graph, which is expressed in visual images. Let us consider these in the light of Beckett's ritual impulses and the choices he made for his absurdist expression.

When Pozzo and Lucky return in the second part of the play, Pozzo is blind and Lucky is dumb. The situation increases dependency for both master and servant, and perhaps this is the reason why Lucky could not be sold at the slave market. However, we must remember that Lucky is the underdog, and if anybody should be saved it ought to be him. Rather, as servant and a dumb individual, his situation has worsened and, compared to his master whose blindness has hardly humbled him, Lucky seems to be the worse off. Furthermore, Godot, the anticipated personage (hope, savior, need), has not come. In two instances, one foreshadowing the other, the Boy supposed to be a servant of Godot (his identity as Godot's servant is hardly certain) promises his master would be there the following day. Consequently, by all intents and purposes, salvation is uncertain.

Other images evoked by this thematic statement become apparent. For instance, the image of the hopelessness of waiting, when Gogo and Didi suggest they leave but remain motionless and do nothing. But more crucial is the image at the third stage of the thematic graph, the image of hopeless existence, when humanity gives "birth astride a grave . . ."[9] First expressed by Pozzo in frustrated anger, it is parroted a few minutes later, more evocatively, by the despair of Vladimir:

> Astride of a grave and a difficult birth. Down in the hole, lingeringly, the gravedigger puts on the forceps. We have time to grow old. The air is full of our cries . . . I can't go on."[10]

We may then recollect and connect. At the beginning of the play, Vladimir has walked in through a passage with feet astride (of a grave?).[11]

As a final example in this chapter, let can consider a woman playwright whose ritual impulses, as a woman, not only describes the metaphysical enigma of the creative process, but gives expression to their metaphysical ordering.

In the preface to her collection, *The America Play and Other Works*, Suzan-Lori Parks variously lets us into the ritual impulses of her creative process[12]. For her, theater in a symbiotic relationship with life is an arena for rewriting history, for within this microcosmic site of life are historical artifacts of the dead to be investigated, dug out and evaluated. Her objective as an African American playwright, therefore, is to locate the African American ancestral burial ground (the metaphysical site of her creative process) and, through ritual immersion, "dig for bones, find bones, hear the bones sing, write it down."[13] Her plays are therefore, like a historical fact, an interpretive realization of the ancestral bones, that is, the African American characteristic and cultural experience. Furthermore, the structural pattern of the plays gives us an idea of the exact nature of her creative ordering.

The creative/historical recall, as she implies, is by no means absolute since it must be considered one person's interpretation—as history should be considered. On the other hand, the process, like all creativity, is not an easy one; as such, in an effort to set the facts/artifacts straight, the ritual struggle involves repetition and revision. Ms. Parks rightly exemplifies the expression and structure of the process with those of jazz music, the probable source of her inspiration or Muse. In terms of what we have established, jazz music is her psychic vehicle of ritual with which she, the priestess/ritualist, approaches the powers of the metaphysical space or arena for certain knowledge.[14]

Perhaps a play of hers that best demonstrates this ritual struggle is *The America Play*, a perfect example for establishing the ritual impulses that manifest Ms. Park's dramatic expression and structure. True to her "muse-ic," her inspiration power of expression, the construct follows that of jazz rendition, rather than the usual dramatic-action structure—although a thread of an action is eventually discernible. First, the thematic idea or premise of the work is established like a jazz introductory sequence or theme. Then, through repetition and revision, what she calls "rep and rev," this idea-note is developed and becomes progressively concretized. Also, like in *Waiting for Godot*, the thematic idea follows a graph.

In the expressive process of *The America Play*, idea-subject-theme-action, all in one, aligns with Suzan-Lori Parks' concept of theater as a metaphysical arena for making history. A particular history (which, by extension, replicates all historical facts) is in question, a history that concerns the African American experience. Ms. Parks shies away from any specific meaning of the black experience, so as not to be misunderstood and not to compartmentalize the experience into a reductionist perception of it. However, she acknowledges that the experience is a microcosmic history that has been "unrecorded, dismembered, washed out" creating a hole in the macrocosmic history of America.

Significantly Ms. Parks expresses a physical and metaphorical grave being dug up, for artifacts that might shed light on and reconstruct the facts of an African American ancestry. Thus, while the idea of the play questions the validity of the "Greater" American history, it validates the equally significant "Lesser" African-American. The playwright concretizes this idea of the greater and the lesser by presenting us with contrasting images of her central character, called the Foundling Father, and Abraham Lincoln, a Founding Father—whose characteristics the Foundling Father (a look-alike) assumes and exploits as an actor. Launching the images as the subject of the play, like an introductory theme-phrase in music, the playwright uses the contrasts to deepen our perception of the Foundling Father, who and what he is, through the jazzy thematic variation-detail of repetition and revision. The details we receive about the Foundling Father are the given circumstances that nurture the playwright's ritual impulses used to develop the thematic idea of the play and the de-emphasized objective-action.

We gather that the Foundling Father was once a gravedigger by profession, and had a wife, LUCY, and a son, BRAZIL, who supported his funerary family business. Leaving his family, he went out west in pursuit of a compelling ambition—acting. As an actor in theme parks, the Foundling Father capitalized on his abilities to impersonate great men of American history, such as Abraham Lincoln, whose close resemblance he bore. Most especially, he re-enacted moments in history that called attention to the greatness of the historical figures. His favorite delineation and enactment (excerpts of which he and the playwright ritualize throughout the play) was the assassination of Lincoln while watching a play at the Ford Theater. As the excerpts reveal, visitors to the park who wish to participate in the act pay a penny, assume the assassin, John Wilkes Booth, select from a choice of provided pistols, stand in position, then shoot the blanks. The guffawing Lincoln character then "slumps in his chair."[15]

These are the given circumstances, what I call idea-narrative. Through the playwright's ritual "rep and rev" style, these given circumstances (vocational grave-digging, ambition pursuits, character impersonation, and assassination-acts) gradually assume a deeper and clearer perception, especially in Act Two. They become metaphoric impulses, ritualized to put a question on historical facts, such that make Lincoln a "Great Man" and the Foundling Father a "Lesser Known," especially with the implication of the similarities that exist between the two. The Great Man, a Founding Father, was by trade a President, and the Lesser Known, the Foundling Father, was by trade a gravedigger —Founding ironically contrasts Foundling, a forgotten, a castaway, an underdog. On second thoughts, both are positions of self-worth and conditions of survival, driven by opportunism—one by the status-building opportunism of politics, and the other by the socio-economic opportunism of acting. In fact, both representations presuppose a kind of political fakery. There is also an implication that both men died in similar ways—the Foundling Father might have been shot with real bullet during one of his acts. Furthermore, both men died during a theatrical event—one, who favored equality for all, died witnessing the theatrical event; the other, who used his delineation to express equality for all, died performing the theatrical event. To get the full picture, we will have to take into consideration the probable cause that drove the assailants of both men to their horrible deeds—racism.

The idea-narrative of Act One, which expresses the thematic-subject of "history," gives us all we need to know about the Foundling Father—his vocation, ambition, and capacities as an artist—all in contrast with what we know of Abraham Lincoln. The details represent certain facts and fiction of history. In a way, they are products of the ritual immersion that the playwright needs to experience (the brooding or gestation stage of the creative process) after the initial idea-note has struck the playwright's creative psyche—that is, before committing to the physical stage of writing. Here, Ms. Parks seems to have recorded in writing this process of thought, with its shifting sequences of repetition and revision.

Act Two develops the thematic-subject of history, or of historical truths. This is the present time of the play, when the past is brought to the present, the thematic aligns with the dramatic, and history and the act of digging receive their fuller and metaphoric meaning. At the possible site of the Foundling Father's grave, Lucy and Brazil are digging for the artifacts of his acting profession, with the view to finding out about him and how he might have died. In order words, they are digging out the past, the remembrance, or the possible history of the Foundling Father. In the process, they demonstrate the family's funerary business in which Brazil was the weeping mourner, and Lucy was "Confidence," the person to which the dying, before their death, confided the "secret" last word[16]. At the site of digging, both Brazil and Lucy put their professional expertise to work in an effort to reconstruct the truth of the Foundling Father—Brazil weeping, and Lucy straining her ears to the wind, perchance to hear the probable final word.

In fact, some kind of history seems to be in the making, and the process seems to connect with Lori Parks' idea of questionable history—digging for artifacts suggests a kind of researching process for historical facts. Such research also applies to delineation of characters, a role-research that the Foundling Father must have done in order to represent his delineated characters to the hilt. Implicit in these processes, which Lucy and Brazil are experiencing in the present, are the painstaking and frustrating efforts of research, interpretation and verbal expression—efforts exerted to understand, and to record or create facts. Brazil intimates: "We got Daddy's ways, Daddy's got ours. When there's no Confidence available, we just dribble thuh words out. In uh whisper."[17] In other words, when there were no available facts, they invented or faked them.

Also implicit is the difficult task of recording facts of history, or any fact at all—for any reconstruction of probable truth is liable to fabrication and invention, resulting in a problematic gap that Ms. Park indicates as "the Great Hole of History."[18] This tendency applies to any interpretation at all, whether creative or factual, and Ms Parks clarifies the notion for us in her preface: "Since history is a recorded or remembered event, theater, for me, is a perfect place to "make history. . ."[19]

Ms. Parks also realizes the thematic graph of history (acquisition of history, and the process of research and interpretation) in textual structure. Entitled THE HALL OF WONDERS, Act Two, the present time of the play, is broken into the following divisions: "Big Bang" (that is, the problem or the mystery) "Echo" (the strife to understand) "Archeology" (available research, study or evidence) "Spadework" (digging or researching for facts) "Echo" (the attempt to interpret) "The Great Beyond" (interpretation, invention, fabrication). Hence, assumptions of history or of truth may not be regarded as absolute.

The thematic questions that Ms. Parks seems to be asking all along with her thematic-idea of history become obvious. For instance, the historical reality that calls attention to Abraham Lincoln as a "Great Man," is it worthy of honor and fame any more than the reality that surrounds the Foundling Father's profession, the "Lesser Known"? Is the fact of history any more truthful than the truth of a role-playing? Or, for that matter, the historical reconstructions of the "Great Man," are they any less inconsistent or less fake, than the theatrical exploits or the fake-art of the Foundling Father? In "thuh hall. Of. Wonders", which suggests Hall of Fame, archives, museum, or document (and *The America Play* is one such document), Ms. Parks resolves her ritual impulses (thematic-subject, thematic-idea, thematic-graph) by placing the two men's greatness side by side along with the artifacts that characterize their greatness.

The chapter has focused, at times indirectly, on what constitutes a dramatic structure—that is, matters of subject, theme and action of a play. These components I have argued as the impulses that the playwright employs, consciously or otherwise, to develop, ritualize or dramatize his or her play. These impulses are part of the ongoing creative process, once the idea or note (muse-ic) strikes the creative psyche, a process that results in the dramatic expression. As we can see from the different plays used as illustration (from the formality of the classical plays to the deconstructing preoccupations of the contemporary plays) these impulses vary in the way they affect the playwright to express himself or herself. The following chapter will focus on the expressive factor that helps the playwright connect these impulses in order to develop his or her dramatic endeavor.

NOTES

1. See "The Fourth Stage," in *Myth, Literature and the African World*.
2. See Corrigan, *The Theater in Search of a Fix*, 21.
3. The phrase is Oscar Brockett's. See *History of the Theatre*, 9th edition, 21; also *The Theater: An Introduction*, 2nd edition (NY: Holt, Rinehart and Winston, Inc., 1969), 81–82.
4. Martin Esslin also expresses this thought. See *Theatre of the Absurd*, 32–34.
5. *Waiting for Godot*, 8–9.
6. *Godot*, 28–29.
7. *Godot*, 28.
8. See *The Theater of the Absurd*, 34-35.
9. *Waiting for Godot*, 57.
10. *Godot*, 58.
11. *Godot,* 7.
12. Suzan-Lori Parks, *The America Play and Other Works* (New York: Theatre Communications Group, Inc., 1995), 3–22.
13. *The America Play*, 4.
14. Interestingly, Ms. Parks implies this by her observation on possession. See "Possession" in *The America Play*, 4–5.

15. See *The America Play*, 164.
16. *The America Play*, 162; 176–177; 179.
17. *The America Play*, 177.
18. *The America Play*. See 179–182.
19. *The America Play*, 4.

Chapter Four

Visible Dramatic Vehicle and Its Ritual Implications: The Central Character

We must continue to go back to our premise. An idea is born in the psyche of the playwright, an idea in need of visual and physical concreteness. Through a ritual struggle to interpret it, the idea evokes an image that is pregnant with dramatic possibilities, which the playwright explores with a conceived or proposed central character and the objective of that character. Whether or not the playwright outlines the impulses (of situation, theme and plot) that eventually structure his or her expression, the playwright plunges into an abyss of uncertainties, and it is only through a force of creative will (the commitment to the objective of writing) he or she realizes the physical expression. However, it is a commitment and will that has origins in the idea that struck.

To exemplify and understand this dramatic will, let us once again consider Wole Soyinka's explication of the ritual process in which the hero-god Ogun (principle of creativity, and archetype of creative-artist) flounders in the abyss of uncertainties in his objective to forge (create) a passage of understanding between god and human. According to Soyinka, it is only through combative will that the artist-hero (by extension, any creative artist) survives the annihilating forces of the abyss of creativity and realizes his objective.

Ogun's objective is to make divine-metaphysical connections, on behalf of the other gods, with human-physical counterparts. The creative artist's objective is to make physical connections, on behalf of the human-community, with his or her psychical (metaphysical) impressions regarding the nature of things. The playwright's objective, on behalf of his or her audience-community, is to concretize those psychical impressions in visual-dramatic terms and with human presence so that the playwright can communicate the message about the nature of things.

To plunge into the creative abyss, the creative artist needs an impetus, that which in turn compels the combative will that challenges the annihilating forces that seem to obstruct the realization of the desired objective. Ogun's impetus is his own individuality as actor/motivator, which wields an implement (a representation of Ogun's conviction and action), that is, the machete he forged to help realize his objective—both the machete and Ogun are one as metal-symbol and metal-god. The playwright's actor/motivator is his or her central character fused with the playwright's individuality, wielding an implement and representation of his or her belief and action, that is, the playwright's monotonic (singular), dramatic voice—which constitutes a monologue or a dialogue as the case may be. I shall discuss the nature of this monotonic implement in the next chapter.

With the image of the central character (whether tentative or definitive) clearly perceived in an action, the playwright's voice receives the power needed to motivate and stimulate the ritual impulses of situation, subject, theme and plot, although the playwright is not fully conscious of them at first. This power, not to be confused with "muse-ic" (the power that conceives the idea and liberates and sustains the voice) has to do with action. The stronger the playwright's conviction of his or her objective vis-a-vis the central character's, the more impactive is the playwright's voice, and the more determined the playwright/central-character's combative will confronts any obstacles opposing the objective.

Thus, the central character is the motivating agent or ritual vehicle of the playwright's expression, invented to help plunge the playwright into the abyss of unknown to wrestle with the dramatic potential of the idea-note, and subsequently help resolve the dilemma in which the playwright finds himself or herself—that is, the uncertainties that confront playwright's objective of expressing the dramatic idea-note. The previous chapter discusses how the objective of the central character aligns with the objective of the playwright. Here, the aligned objective is already conceived, and the central character is ready to serve the playwright and ritualize his or her drama. The question is what is the dramatic potential of that objective?

The annihilating forces that confront the creative artist, in this case the playwright, are the uncertainties of realization the playwright faces in the abyss of creativity, the so-called problems challenging the validity of playwright/central-character's abysmal plunge. These forces raise questions, or, as it turns out to be, perhaps they are challenged by the very questions raised. For, possible answers to the questions not only reinforce the combative will of the playwright/central-character to struggle on, they increase the ability of the playwright to invent. The initial questions likely to confront the playwright are: What do you want, and what does your character want in order to express what you want? In other words, what is the objective of the central character, and what are his or her likely obstacles? Possible answers to those questions give the playwright and central character the initial dramatic thrust to cracking the idea-kernel, so to speak, and expressing its contents. Similar thrusts will develop from answers to other annihilating questions that seem to diminish the confidence or the commitment of the playwright/central character to the objective, questions such as: What is the situation of the moment? How is the central character reacting to it? How consistent is the reaction to the central character's objective? Does this reaction indicate a character trait of the central character?

In my playwriting classes, I demonstrate how these questions are initiated by making the students relate to the given circumstances of a situation: John needs five hundred dollars. The money was a debt he had incurred some months before to take care of some business, and which he had promised to pay back immediately. Well, he had not, and now his debtor is nipping at his heels. Shakespeare dealt with such a situation, resulting in his play *The Merchant of Venice*. Without going into the intricacies of Shakespeare's play, we proceed with the situation. John approaches a friend Marcus to borrow the money to pay off his debt. John knows that Marcus has the money to spare, but the problem is Marcus is tight-fisted and therefore is unwilling to lend. Questions arise: How is John going to persuade Marcus to give him the money? What kind of person is John himself? All these are pertinent to the persuasive strategies he must device to achieve his objective of borrowing five hundred dollars from Marcus.

The parameters of a possible drama are set in this simple incident. When I taught acting, I had often proposed such a situation for improvisation—one student is the borrower and the other is the potential lender. The lender was instructed to make it difficult for the borrower, so that the borrower would have to invent strategies to get the money. It was up to the lender to give or not give, depending on whether he or she was persuaded sufficiently. This exercise is similar to the playwright's, or to the action the playwright describes for his or her characters through questions raised. John's objective (and the playwright's) is to find a way to get the money from Marcus. Obtaining the money is John's need, but it also defines the action of the play, what John does to try to achieve his objective, which may or may not be realized. The achievement, or non-achievement, is consequent to a number of factors in spite of John's strategies. There are many ways that John can obtain the money, or many options open to the playwright. John, depending on his character, must choose what is possible, or what is most effective for him. The playwright, depending on character traits of his central character, will discover the options that best serve his or her character. The options chosen implicate the questions asked.

John may decide to proceed indirectly, flattering Marcus before telling him his troubles, hoping to spur Marcus's generosity. If Marcus fails to respond positively to this strategy (and this reaction may take any form of his supposed stinginess), John may decide on a more direct approach, demanding the money from Marcus, probably as a favor due. Again, Marcus may not be moved. If anything Marcus may believe John owes him, since he's bailed John out of many scrapes before—or so he sees it. John may then go even further, as a desperate man, to blackmail Marcus. Various circumstances can factor into the strategy, including love-relationships, their professions, even the very nature of their friendship, all depending on how desperate and unscrupulous John is or how adamant is Marcus' stinginess. In terms of playwriting, relevant questions posed by the playwright regarding the central character will develop the objective action, conflict and characteristics of the central character as the dramatic vehicle of the playwright's expression.

In these sequences of action we have in fact come upon matters of character and personal stakes; let us hold these for the moment to make a significant point about dramatic objective and action. Frequently, as prospective writers of drama, we have misunderstood what the action of the play is. It has nothing to do with the various physical actions that characters perform, such as walking up to a table and picking up the vase, or patting another character by the shoulder, or the various "wars" characters often engage in. Some of these are of course important choices or reactions but are irrelevant if they have nothing to do with the central action of the play. This action is the first thing actors (as physical interpreters of the text) often wish to find out in order to decide the relationship of their own objectives to the action. Otherwise, choices of action made cannot be described, that is, truthfully—a qualifier actors love to acknowledge.

The action of the play, therefore, has to do with characters' objectives; to be able to relate to these effectively, the central action need be defined. It is the center or through line that a director must define clearly before he or she begins to express it on stage-space, or the direction that the actor must find and relate to in order to motivate his or her character-goals. All of this, of course, points to the playwright and the clarity of his or her expression. In other words, the directing process ultimately identifies the playwright, how clearly he or she has perceived that objective-action. It is the action that is concretized from the initial voice-note or the idea-kernel into a physical image, a situation, and then to the objective-action. The central character emerges as the single ritual vehicle of that action, from the play's point of attack (when the action is visible to the central character) to climax and resolution.

However, although the playwright knows his or her central character and that character's objective, the playwright does not have to be conscious of the process of development. In other words, the playwright could express his or her play at the initial stage of writing through intuition. In fact, the organic approach of this book encourages such intuitive ordering of creativity. But ultimately, the intuitive process must give way to a more conscious and practical process, the trial and error of the first draft must submit to a critical engagement, which allows the playwright to see any intuitive obfuscation and to give his or her expression better focus and clarity. It is the interpretive clarity the ritual high priest must eventually give, with a conscious objectivity, to his possessed utterance from the *illud tempus*. Like the high priest, the more the experience of the playwright, the more critical perception he or she is able to lend his or her expression.

To give a more practical illustration, it is likely that, at the initial exploring phase, the idea-note gets distorted, changes perspective, reconstructs itself a thousand times before yielding its true image, and therefore its expressive structure. The stage of exploration may also create in the playwright a funny, woozy feeling of helplessness that the grasp of creativity might not be achieved. With no perceivable light at the end of the tunnel, a kind of disillusionment may follow the frustration, a wish to abandon the project altogether. It is a moment of uncertainty during the playwright's ritual immersion in the metaphysical space, a moment that seeks affirmation and a definition of the idea-note that struck, or the muse-ic that compels the playwright's voice to interpret and express.

Thus disengaged as if from the physical state of awareness or consciousness, the playwright flounders in the metaphysical abyss, like Soyinka's primal artist, Ogun, or, perhaps more conceivable in Western imagination, like a Dionysiac satyr-Thespis thumping a frenetic jig in order to make manifest the image of Dionysus. In the struggle to sustain individuality, and therefore secure a hold on a creative/dramatic quest, the probing playwright, like the ritual artist-archetypes before him, must summon up his or her combative will. For only the power of conviction, the affirmation of his muse-ic, can rescue the playwright from the feeling of disillusionment or annihilation threatening his or her creative capacity. Only through sheer commitment to the force of will can the playwright finally see the shape of his or her emerging drama. That power, that force of will, resides in the playwright's central character and that character's objective.

But, merely perceiving the central character and that character's objective does not mean the playwright has total grasp of his or her expression. The playwright's standing may be stronger, more secure and positive, but he or she may need ritual re-immersion of the metaphysical space, only this time, the playwright becomes more confident of results, of giving shape to his or her dramatic expression. It is re-immersion, perhaps anticipating a second draft, that aims at modifying or focusing the formerly amorphous rendering of the idea-note, providing some form and clarity to the image and action expressed. However, the re-immersion may still be a phase in the ritual ordering of the creative process, prior to giving consideration to the fine-tuning of technique, a deliberation that may also required several revisions.

The process of immersion and re-immersion anticipates elements of technique that fine-tunes the expression of the playwright. These fundamental elements are what gives the central character its power, and what helps the playwright recover the confidence that would help achieve his or her expression.

Fundamental Elements of Drama:

Crucial to the objective action of the central character are the fundamental but essential elements of drama, the agents that serve the playwright and his or her central character, the ritual vehicle of the playwright's expression. Robert Benedetti, in his *The Actor at Work* rightly enumerates these four elements, which, as we will see, are determined from the point of view of the central character: [1]

1. Conflict: What places in doubt the resolution of an objective—the obstacles that confront the central character, creating conflict.
2. Personal stakes: Conditions that compel the choices the central character makes in engaging his or her objective. We can assume that the greater or the more compelling the condition, the more involved is the central character with the objective.
3. Urgency or Deadline: The certain time the central character, by circumstances of events, is required to accomplish his or her objective. Again, we can assume that the shorter and closer the deadline, tighter the schedule, the more crucial it is for the central character to achieve his objective of resolving a present crisis, and therefore the more desperate the character becomes. However, it must be understood that deadlines and consequent desperation can come in various ways, blatant or subtle.
4. Commitment to action: The consistency of the character's commitment to his or her objective-action. Personal stakes and deadline, of course, make this commitment more insistent.

These are the basic elements of drama. They can readily be seen executed on commercial television (soap operas and sitcoms) and in movies, where they were often exploited to engage the sensibilities of the audience, at times to melodramatic excess. In good drama, they are explored, but often more subtly that they are sometimes not easy to perceive. We can begin to understand these elements by locating them in drama, from the easily detectable situations to ones more subtly dramatized. The playwright may intuitively respond to and take advantage of them as he or she gives expression to his or her drama. But to be aware of them increases the playwright's ritual power to make crucial dramatic choices. First, let us pursue these elements in the example given earlier regarding John and Marcus.

John needs to borrow five hundred dollars from Marcus to pay off an old debt. We can intensify that situation by adding specific circumstances more crucial to John's objective of borrowing. John is already two months behind in paying his rent. John gambles, and he has gambled away the money he could have used to pay at least part of his debt, hoping he could win a jackpot at the casino. With third month rent approaching, John faces possible eviction and further problems this would incur. These are John's *personal stakes* and why he badly needs to borrow the money. The stakes increase if his eviction is imminent. A *conflict* is raised when John approaches Marcus for help and Marcus proves difficult—not what John expects. As such, the realization of John's objective (getting the five hundred dollars) is in doubt. Perhaps the landlord has sent John the eviction notice, so he has a *deadline*, which intensifies every day, every hour, every minute. Perhaps the urgency has spanned over three days, then two, then one, and the landlord has called the police—so John has become more and more desperate. When it was a matter of three days, or two, or even one, there was still some time, and the situation might be averted if he were lucky with the slot machines or with poker at the casino. But now, that illusory possibility is closed, and the drama intensifies. John is at the end of his tether when he approaches Marcus. This situation forces him to be desperately committed to his objective of getting money from Marcus, by whatever means necessary—hence his various dire strategies. Now let us consider these elements at work in three plays.

First, the old faithful, *Oedipus Rex*. As has been indicated severally in this book, Oedipus's objective is to find out the truth. This truth involves the death of the old king, Laius, and Oedipus's own identity, that is, the rather nebulous facts of his birth and parentage that has hounded him all his life. In fact, the stakes of discovering the truth are high for Oedipus, first, because of the plague ravaging his city and subjects. More than this, through a past circumstance, he has been identified as a riddle solver, a seeker and finder of truth—he had found out the truth behind the riddle of the Sphinx. Thus, he is expected to discover the truth of the new puzzle—Laius's death and the mysteries surrounding it. Furthermore, true to his compulsive nature, Oedipus commits everybody, including himself, to a curse-ridden oath to punish anyone who knows or has clues to the truth but refuses to tell. As part of his action of finding out the truth, this proclamation is the ultimate stake that puts pressure on Oedipus.

The situation for Oedipus is urgent for a number of reasons. First, his subjects are dying and crying out to him for help. But other facts evolve complicating the situation. Apollo, through message of his oracle at Delphi and the message-carrier, Creon, compounds the death riddle with another riddle—there is an unnamed killer at large, whose detection and banishment is crucial to eradicating the plague. Further, accusations of the crime are mud-slung between Oedipus and Creon, to such an extent that Oedipus is compelled to validate his indictment on Creon and clear his own good name. Along with this are Oedipus's feelings of guilt, roused by Teiresias's pronouncement that he, Oedipus, was not only the killer of Laius, but also the one whose fated identity has already been realized and is headed for catastrophe. Because of these prodding accusations and doubts, which create obstacles (conflicts) to Oedipus's pursuit of truth, there is an implied deadline to his objective. It seems he must decipher the truth from all suggested and opposing facts immediately, if he is to avoid certain madness. Hence, his commitment to his objective, even if it reveals the truth that might implicate him. At any rate, he has involved himself in consequences right from the beginning. He has included himself in a curse-directed oath that is hanging over anyone hiding the truth of the killer of Laius. To know that truth, which may either absolve or damn Oedipus, is a critical issue for Oedipus, one that needs to be resolved, if the city is to be saved from the raging plague.

All Oedipus's actions, that is, the choices he makes in his objective, are of course relative to his character, reinforced by his conflicts, stakes, deadline and commitment. Impulsive, rash, quick to anger, prideful, quick to jump to conclusions, blind to reason, Oedipus allows his ego to intoxicate and propel him and his objective to catastrophe. That ego, made emphatic by the dramatic factors, also creates his greatest conflict, since it obstructs his vision to see other people's truth about his objective and, inversely, to see his own destructive objective. Such blindness is the flaw of most classical tragic heroes, but it implicates their tragic heroism—that is, the *hubris* (that defiant arrogance of conviction) that backs up the flaw. In fact, it is the stuff that makes every individual, potentially, a tragic hero.

While on Oedipus's egotistic compulsion, we may recall that Othello faces similar circumstantial problems in his commitment to an objective of justifying his actions against Desdemona, and absolving his tainted reputation. Like Oedipus, actions are driven by his ego, characterized by a compulsive yet myopic vision based on his limited knowledge of the "truth" told by others such as Iago. As such, he also is his own biggest conflict, and similarly, the stakes of absolving himself are high—he has a reputation as a veritable and just commander; he has defended his honor of love to the world in the court of Venice; he, true to his greatness, has demonstrated his abilities as a winning warrior in Cyprus; most important, he has found himself in a bind of jealousy to seek an "ocular proof." Thus driven like Oedipus, Othello is unrelenting, and the resolution of his objective becomes catastrophic.

In *Oedipus* and *Othello*, the essential factors of drama, although subtle, are clearly defined. But let us consider them in a play in which they are not that obvious. In *Waiting for Godot*, a play that makes claims contrary to dramatic conventions as we know it, the so-called drama of the undramatic, it is possible to identify these elements.

To all appearances, nothing seems to happen in *Waiting for Godot*. Yet, something does happen, and we can begin to see this by identifying the ritual (dramatic) implements. As already been established, the objective of the two tramps is to wait for Godot. We gather that the figure has a certain significance for their existence, perhaps someone or something that would make their lives more meaningful. Hence, they have personal stakes in waiting and in staying alive, a forbearance that is constantly tested by Godot not showing up, by the frustrations of trying to stay alive, by the despair they often experience when they are short of ideas for the activity that keeps them alive, and by the struggle of their different personalities to tolerate each other's company. These obstacles create conflicts to their objective of waiting and at moments make them consider abandoning the whole idea, except that Godot might come.

The deadline in this play is nebulous, because the characters are constantly redefining it. As tramps, they display an urgent need for better life circumstances. Yet this need always runs counter to the deadline they set themselves, that is, the tomorrow that does not seem to end with the appearance of Godot, or the abandonment of their waiting, or the ending of their lives as they often suggested. Consequently, their persistence in waiting, that is, the commitment to objective-action, outlives the present time of the play. Because it is an absurdist play, Beckett's dramaturgical choice is of course intentional. For, the reality that Beckett's realism paints absurdly neither guarantees expectation nor salvation—hope seems a perpetual and hopeless need to wait for.

Dramatic elements, or ritual implements, make it possible for a play, through its central character or focus, to engage its audience. Even a play whose expression seems very abstract, such as *The America Play* by Susan-Lori Parks, must engage the audience for it to survive as drama. To discover the hidden elements of drama in such a play is to begin to grasp the playwright's meaning and the impulses that serve the playwright in creating his or her dramatic expression. Ms. Parks's play offers such a challenge. In fact, an examination of *The America Play* reiterates an important fact of playwriting

—that a play, although relates to the past in given circumstances, must dramatize the present time of its expression in order to engage its reader or audience. It is the dramatized present time of a play that constitutes its dramatic elements—what the playwright should ultimately seek in order to overcome likely problems of abstraction.

The America Play, as we are led to believe in the first act, dramatizes an abstract concept that expresses itself in the past—the questionable fact of history. In order to relate to the dramatic elements that serve the playwright, we must ask the pertinent question: "Where's the present time of the play?" It appears in act 2, when we realize, by the present action of Brazil and Lucy, that the Foundling Father is already dead. Normally, the present action happening at that time in the play would be too late to engage the audience—that, incidentally, could happen to this play on stage, especially if it is not interpreted and dramatized correctly. However, if the play is to hold the interest of the audience, there should be a sort of dramatic present in the first act, which, as we have seen, is really a narrative of the past. To create this present is the challenge that Ms. Parks could have encountered. How has she resolved it?

In the narrative past, we recognize the Foundling Father, his vocation, and the contrasts he cuts with President Lincoln. But, consciously or not, in order to sustain our interest, Ms. Parks narrates much of that past in the historic present, that is, by bringing into the conscious present the Foundling Father's dramatized skits of the assassination of President Lincoln. But even these, along with the history being narrated, may be ultimately a hard sell, because they tend to be repetitious, and they do not seem to go anywhere other than being a theatrical device. An impatient audience may have become bored and walked out of the theater.

In an effort to engage the interest of the audience, who have been struggling with their attention span to see something happen in the present, the playwright provides the present action and the dramatic potential of act 2— Lucy and Brazil are digging for artifacts at the possible grave of the Foundling Father, artifacts that could shed some light on the success of his impersonation, and on his fame. As established before, while the dug "holes" in this play suggest the holes (gaps) in the historical facts that identify comparable individuals (in this case, as greater and lesser), they also imply the vacuum of inconsistencies created by the dug up, or researched, facts. It is these gaps and inconsistencies that seem to create obstacles, or raise conflicts against the objective-action of Lucy and Brazil—the digging up of facts that may or may not completely resolve the true identity and artistic merit of the Foundling Father. Through our knowledge of the narrative of act 1, and perhaps more to the playwright's intention, the validity or invalidity contrasts those that also put a question mark on historical and political greatness of figures such as Abraham Lincoln. In fact, efforts to understand and resolve the ambiguity, that is, the gaps created by the unknown factor, often result in personal interpretation, which is common in any investigation (historiographical, artistic, archeological, etc.).

The stakes, if not formally defined, are in fact high for Lucy and Brazil. Both characters are compelled by the need to document possible and probable facts of a cultural pater, as it were, facts (African American) which otherwise would lie deeply buried and thus remain unknown or insignificant, as they have been regarded in the past. In fact, this is also Parks's playwriting objective—to document hitherto neglected African American history. As in any investigative endeavor, the struggle to resolve and document facts of the past, and if need be fabricate them, commits Lucy and Brazil to their objective. As previously noted, the playwright also uses the structure, the sectional divisions of act 2, to dramatize the process of the struggle, marking the stages of Lucy and Brazil's interpretive effort. As in Beckett's play, deadline or urgency is a somewhat elusive element, but it is interwoven with the personal stakes of the characters. It is the urgent need to dig and set down what the playwright calls the "dismembered, disjointed" facts of African American history, by implication, a history that is equally important and worthy of recognition as facts of American history.

We have explored the dramatic elements, or ritual implements, of drama in the different plays, not so much to assert their existence as dramatic imperatives; it is to show them as logical dramatic devices useful to the creative sensitivity of the playwright, in the effort to engage the audience. Employing them, psychically or consciously, they help the playwright ritualize (dramatize), on the one hand, the relationship between the objective of the central character and his or her conflicts, and, on the other, the connection between those conflicts and the consequences they bring to bear on the central character as he or she tries to realize objective through action. For instance, because of the personal stakes of reputation and identity precipitating Oedipus' objective of finding out the truth, Sophocles was able to dramatize and engage his audience credibly with Oedipus' consequential struggle against obstacles to his objective. Similarly, Gogo and Didi's objective of waiting for Godot is made more significant and engaging by their personal stakes of bettering their present existence as tramps or underdogs. Their objective, along with the stakes and the characters' commitment to wait, placed against the frustrating obstacles that confront them, make the consequences of their wait a tragedy of the human condition. As for the more abstractly conceived and metaphorically dramatized *The America Play*, the idea-narrative of the first act informs the objective, personal stakes and conflict of Lucy and Brazil in the second act, which dramatizes the frustrations of digging (researching), and the consequences of such processes—a possible biased interpretation of facts.

In fact, Suzan-Lori Parks' play, in relation to her concept of theatre, brings us back to the playwright and the art of playwriting in terms of those dramatic elements. Ms. Parks informs us that she sees the investigative research of historiography in synchronous relationship with the creative process of theatre, vis-a-vis playwriting. Her objective, therefore, is to dig up history, African American history, in a theatrical experience or event. To this extent, the result of her investigative expression is as factual and personal in theatre, as it is in history. In other words, her playwriting, an attempt to reconstruct history, is at once valid and invalid as is a historiographical construct.

Her objective is to record the historical reality that surrounds the African American experience, in an effort to bring the experience up to par with the historical construct that had hitherto excluded it—the written history that had mainly focused and elevated the greatness of White America. The objective, she recognizes, is fraught with obstacles as with all such investigation and documentation—such that Lucy and Brazil demonstrate in their quest for the historical reality that calls attention to the Foundling Father.

As an African American, Ms Parks has personal stakes in reconstructing African American history, an endeavor that is not only necessary but also crucial; hence, Ms. Parks' artistic commitment to it as a playwright is real and consistent. The result is an affirmative placement of the African-American greatness and self-worth side by side with those of White America. If the affirmation seems a contrivance of an artistic license, we should remind ourselves that a personal interpretation is not unknown in any investigative research. In fact, the probable truth lies within the constant revision and repetition (the constant reevaluation) of the factual.

The aforementioned examples of plays, with regard to the dramatic elements, lead us to at least three stylistic approaches to playwriting. In *Oedipus Rex* and *Othello*, the elements dramatize a more formal sequential approach, although they have the potential of engaging various levels of interpretation with the given circumstances. In *Waiting for Godot* on the other hand, the elements ritualize a non-sequential abstraction of given but elusive and interpretive facts, set against a background of isolated void, a hopeless condition of our absurd modern world. In the case of *The America Play*, the abstraction itself, the void, becomes the dramatized expression of probable facts.

The elements of drama therefore seem to be a common dramatic factor in all the plays, although they dramatize the given circumstances differently, and they are not always obvious. At any rate, their presence is very much related to the objective of the central character, the climax of that objective-action, and the consequences the central character faces in pursuing his or her action.

Going back to the original example given above, it is possible to demonstrate that, given the historical and theatrical reality or conventions that condition a playwright, and given the playwright's stylistic bent, a story or a set of given circumstances can be dramatized in various ways.

John's objective is to get five hundred dollars from Marcus at all costs—for if John does not have the money he will be thrown out of the house that very day. Since Marcus is stingy, the question John's objective raises is whether John will be able to persuade Marcus to give him the money. It is an exploitable question that a commercially driven playwright may take advantage of to create an exciting suspenseful drama. He or she may not only increase the stakes for John (the owner of the apartment is connected with the Mob), but also load it with sensational circumstances such as a love affair (John blackmails Marcus with Marcus's extra marital affair). Such devices may woo a wider audience's sense of entertainment.

However, the creative sensibilities of another playwright may need to give the idea of the play an intellectual depth, by using the given circumstances to ritualize a subject that is thought provoking. The operating theme may change from, "A gambling addiction that seeks to rob Peter to pay Paul may result in a dangerous and life-threatening situation" to "Life is a gamble that man continues to challenge with all of his resources." An absurdist playwright, like Beckett, may wish to probe the latter theme more absurdly to show the hopelessness of man's efforts to challenge. This may modify the theme slightly: "Man's challenges of life are a losing gamble." Another playwright, like Suzan-Lori Parks, may wish to dissect the concept of gambling itself, using black characters to investigate it in the history of human experience, as a condition of the survival of the underdog.

Such themes could materialize from the circumstance of John needing to borrow five hundred dollars from Marcus. However, they may also develop from a similar circumstance as ideas probed by the playwright's psyche, ideas which evoke images that gradually concretize a physical and dramatic presence. Whichever way they happen, it is obvious that the themes, through the individual playwright's response to the stimuli of the dramatic elements, will generate different plays and varying roles—depending on the images evoked by each theme, on the social, economic and political inclinations of the playwright, and, of course, on the playwright's stylistic approach.

Whatever the play or the approach, the playwright needs a central focus. He or she also needs to see, at some point, the connection between an objective-action of that focus and the possible consequences of a commitment to that objective-action in the face of many odds, that is, the conflicts raised. This connection is brought about by ritual implements, the essential elements of drama—which may become emphatic in some plays, or tend to be very subtle in others. With these elements, the writing space, or the stage, is set for a physical expression, or a revision of it, an expression that is at once dramatic and theatrical.

NOTES

1. Robert Benedetti, *The Actor at Work*, 4th ed. (NY: Prentice-Hall, Inc., 1986), 5

Chapter Five

Ritual Scope: *The Monologue and the Creative Challenge*

In a dramatic monologue, we encounter a single unadulterated speaker-text. For it is a voice more given to expressing itself openly, untainted and unencumbered by the traps and contraptions of the creative process—that is, the intrusions of other presences that often force a character to wear a mask, thereby making it difficult for the character to be sincere and straightforward with its utterance. However, for the sincerity of the speaker-text to manifest, the voice still has to surmount the inner obstacles it is afflicted with (problems, of idea-imaging, incident-situating, location, character, etc.), except that the voice, with the character it assumes, is answerable to no other voice or character but itself. And if it lies and therefore is insincere, it is lying onto itself. It is the success of its singular triumph over these psychical oppositions that make the monologue a challenging endeavor.

But before going any further, what I mean by a dramatic monologue must be made clear. In its simplest form, it is Hamlet's monologue "To be on not to be . . ." (*Hamlet*, Act 1, sc. 2, lines 56–90) or his "Oh, that too too solid flesh would melt . . ."(*Hamlet*, Act 1, sc. 2, lines 129–159)[1] Such soliloquies describe thought processes that have within them the ingredients of drama. They are not only initiated by a mental crisis that the monologues develop to a climactic accountability and then resolve, but their objective is beleaguered by inner conflicts that are consequential to resolution. For instance, in "To be or not to be," Hamlet's mental crisis is his confused mind, caused by the revelations of his father's ghost, prompting him to contemplate suicide. He therefore analyzes, to himself, the possibility of suicide, to a climactic (really anticlimactic) resolve of non-action. Once again, the accommodation of his reasoning, Hamlet's strong point and yet his weakness (really his hubris), triumphs over any decisive action.

An extension of such soliloquized monologue is the longer, perhaps more complex form, the one character one-act. The likely initial reaction to this form might be to argue that it is hardly a play, since it does not encourage an oppositional, dialogic exchange. In other words, its single character is not confronted by at least another character, a physical presence that challenges his or her objective, raising a conflict whose resolution is in doubt or suspense. Without such a conflict, it would be difficult to define the character's objective-action and its development, which should gravitate towards a climax and therefore a resolution.

Other factors might raise concern—for instance, problems of engaging an audience for a length of time, of lack of physical action, of monotony of movement, and of visual impact. One could think of the difficulties the Greek dramatists might have had in trying to adopt Thespis' ritual dance-drama of one character and the chorus, which led Aeschylus to add another character-actor, and Sophocles yet another, making dramatic interaction more easily achievable.

Because of such problems, the dramatic one-act monologue does pose a challenge to playwrights. However, these difficulties are not insurmountable, for they reflect the problems of playwriting in general. In fact, the challenges of the one-act monologue provide the playwright a grounding of the technicalities of playwriting.

The one-character play, whether one-act or full-length, has gained increasing acceptance as legitimate theater, judging by recent presentational choices of the form on stage. For instance, in National Black Theater Festivals that I have attended since 1989, the number of one-character shows presented has gradually grown from one or two of the earlier festivals, to more than twenty or three quarters of the entire feature in the recent festivals. To be sure, the increase reflects the need to stage a play that is manageable in terms of the cost of showcasing talents. But the increase also indicates a gradual orientation of the audience to the form, all of which makes the understanding of the one-act monologue by the playwright more crucial.

Presentations that have lent credence to the one-character play as a non-drama abound. For instance, the form is often misconceived, resulting in semblances of stand-up comedy, skits, or storytelling. One could perhaps understand why the art of the comedian (whether enacted in skits or a series of jokes) would be attractive to a writer of the one-act monologue, since the audience needed be entertained and engaged somehow. The problem is, the longer such a presentation the more difficult it becomes to hold the attention of the audience. Similarly, the misconception that a one-character play is nothing but a narrative of past events has a dead-end. In terms of drama, what such narratives imply is that the form is merely an exposition of given circumstances—since there is no present time of the play to account for other than the presence of the actor. And if there is no present time, there is no possible avenue for elements of drama to develop an objective-action.

In order for the form to be effective and engaging, the playwright must strive to ritualize the elements that make drama within a present time—it is a basic fact that must be understood. Once the playwright locates this present moment (as opposed to the past of given circumstances) he or she can proceed to focus the objective of the central character in terms of the ritual implements of drama. Of course, this process in the creative experience presupposes the initial psychical idea-note that struck, and its subsequent physical concretization into an image, within which the possibility of a dramatic expression is perceived. Let us retrace our steps.

The monologue, as a physical dramatic expression, is the closest form in the creative process to the single, unvoiced idea that strikes a dramatic note in the creative psyche. What the monologue attempts to do is voice (that is, define and explore) that idea-note in all its purity in a monotone, uncomplicated (at first at any rate) by any other voice or voices that seek to challenge the single voice's purity and tonal priorities. Of course the single voice encounters challenges, physical and internal, but not those issued by other voices that struggle to express their own objectives, peculiarities and priorities, such that develop a two or three or multiple-character play.

When the note-idea evolves in the psyche, or the voice in the deep recesses of the throat, the challenge of the playwright/singer, whose intentions is to render a monologic/monotonic expression of it, lies in giving it a dramatic form. Since the expression is meant for an audience, it must engage that audience, with tonal color, pace, and modulation, as well as with its muse-ic or evocative power of imagination. But perhaps the biggest initial challenge (what distinguishes the playwright from a real singer or a stand-up comedian) is the fact of what determines the character of the voice, and to whom the voice/character is relating. Even if the character of the voice happens to be that of the playwright, in other words, if it is biographical, that character is subject to creative and dramatic change in terms of the character's need or objective—which the playwright should be prepared to experience, and to respond to. And even if the playwright chooses to have the character address the theater audience, the playwright still has to understand the nature and significance of that audience—that is, whom the audience represents. This audience-challenge, of course, need not be taken up right away, but it cannot be ignored.

In my graduate playwriting class where I usually used the monologue exercise, the students almost always assume the audience of the play to be the audience of the theater so that they have their character address the audience directly with certain indifference. Again, it must be emphasized that this approach is possible. Hamlet, after all (consistent to the conventions of his time) supposedly addresses the theater audience, for instance, in his famous soliloquy, "To be, or not to be". But in fact, as with most soliloquies, Hamlet is addressing the audience of his mind; the theater audience just happens to be eavesdropping, so to speak.

Even if the playwright chooses to have the character directly address the theater audience, the playwright needs to imagine and represent that audience specifically in order to avoid problems arising from the playwright's oversight—such as, questions likely to be raised by the theater audience. For the art of drama, after all, is realistic (like real)—that is, drama is not real life, only a representation of aspects of life in a certain form. By identifying a specific audience, which becomes the ideal or stage audience, the monologue creates an artistic distance between the ideal and the real audience. This choice enables the monologue to realize a dramatic life of its own, a magic of its own, its illusion of reality, in short, its realism.

Actually, an expression of any idea-note or voice, be it for a one-act monologue, or for a more extensive exploration of a full-length play, need not at first be more than a simple "monotonic" monologue—monotonic in the sense that it emerges like a pure, unadulterated, full-bodied tone. As stated, this vocal sound, or tone, is the closest in analogy to the intuitive image evoked from the idea that struck the psyche. However, the image/tone is loaded, and, like a soliloquy, the uncluttered voice bares itself out, that is, expresses its thoughts, concerns and apprehensions, usually about something that is critical to its existence or survival. An interpretive analogy of this expressive monotone brings to mind an acting exercise—intoning a difficult speech with eyes closed. The acting exercise not only enables the actor to register and control the direction of breath from the diaphragm, but, more importantly, allows the voicer to hear and secure the meaning and value of the words, unencumbered by inflection. In such a single directional attitude to registration, the playwright/singer is alert and more sensitive to various emotional conditions open to the monotone. For instance, the voice might register a feeling of concern or a disagreement with an individual as close as a friend, or as distant as a political leader. It might recall a pain as tragic as the loss of a spouse or lover, emote a frustration to an incident as serious as any threat to the world's survival, or might be tickled by a joke as comical and ridiculous as the pursuit of an impossible dream like a church rat.

Any such sensations or ideas might surface, seeking consideration in the monotonic attitude of the soliloquy. Since such registers often tend to be one's honest and true feelings, straight from the deep recesses of the conscience, their evocation or vocalization in a soliloquy should prove a worthy class exercise as an initial impetus to dramatic writing. Even if the expression is beset by conflicts (and it is wholesome that the voicer/playwright considers the yeas and nays of an emoted opinion or action—Hamlet's soliloquy indicates such considerations) the obstacles, coming from the same individual, are inner conflicts, unadulterated by an external conflict created by the presence of other characters, voices whose right to equally exist can only complicate the validity of the single individual's right to a free expression.

But we are at the heart of a controversial artistic belief in playwriting. There is evidence to support the fact that the different characters of a play represent the different voices that speak to the playwright. Yet, it can be contended that a play, whether a one-act with one or several characters, or a full-length with many incidents involving complex objectives, originates, more often than not, from a single voice of the playwright. It can be argued that the character or characters that express themselves in dialogue, even though they act like different personalities, ultimately come from the creative inventiveness of a single monologic/monotonic voice, that the individual voice has merely expressed its various facets and characteristics which, however, are limited to the capabilities and the experiences of the playwright. In other words, the seemingly individual characters of the play are traits that the playwright is capable of expressing, traits which, quite naturally, are compelled by the playwright's own potential. For instance, many of my friends that profess to know me very well have found the different me not only in the characters of my plays, but also in the dialogue. In a recent production of a play of mine, which is situated in the U.S. and which evokes African-American characters, the director, a very good friend, woke me up to a probable truth—that even though the play seemed to bear an African-American outlook, it was still very African. While she was not completely correct, because there were other experiential factors to be taken into consideration, what she said was not without some truth.

The proposition about the singular playwright-voice supports my own argument, that the other voices that seem to inform the playwright, dramatizing his or her idea, are adulterated or hypothesized simulations of the singular voice. This does not mean that the playwright cannot experience these voices truthfully. In fact, since they ultimately emanate from the playwright, he or she must continue to define the truth of each and every one of them. The playwright must continue to listen to these voices in order to identify each with the "other" within the playwright's experience; he or she must consequently strive at every turn to modify the character-voice's viewpoint until the playwright is satisfied with consistency and verisimilitude. Regarding this truth, or the accurate impression of each character's individuality, it is pertinent to note the crucial fact of the "other"—that he or she derives from the playwright's encounters with voices or characters within the playwright's experience. Consequently, the voices or the characters could be said to materialize as simulations of the monologic/monotonic voice of the playwright. They are experiences within an experience, that is, simulated features in the ongoing physical articulation of the playwright's idea. With this clarification, let's go back to the voice of the monologue.

When the expression of the one-character play first emerges as the untainted voice of a soliloquized monologue, the initial nondescript voice is instantly challenged by a number of questions, such as: Who is the monologue addressing? Who is the speaker of the monologue? Where is the speaker located? What is the present time of the monologue? What is going on in this present time, which should help focus the objective-action of the speaker? These legitimate questions confronting the playwright are crucial to ritualizing the playwright's creative and dramatic response. My contention is that, to be able to answer these questions, which enable the successful development of the initial monotonic/monologic voice into a one-character one-act, is to be able to meet the challenges of playwriting as a whole, be it in form of a normal one-act or a full-length. In other words, the process of development through these questions offers a fundamental key to the technique of playwriting. Let us deliberate on these challenges by identifying the questions one by one.

THE AUDIENCE

Whom does the monologue address? Or who is the audience, that is, the "stage audience," to which the character/speaker is directing his or her monologue? As stated, it is easy for a playwright, especially a beginner, to overlook this, but if not resolved, it becomes a problem for the actor, the agent for the physical expression of the monologue.

Reasons for possible oversight are quite evident, or can be argued. In traditional plays, dialogue often occurs between at least two people. In that situation, the question of the stage audience is seldom raised—although the identity of the audience, its character, should be understood. In a monologue, of one or multiple acts, it is easy to assume that the audience is present as usual, but it soon becomes clear that it is not, or that the auditorium audience is assumed as the stage audience. Actually, it might very well address the auditorium audience, but the question the playwright must answer is: What particular reason does the speaker have for addressing the monologue to that audience? If the playwright can answer that question, he or she will understand the difference between a theater audience and a stage audience, each of which has its own function.

The auditorium audience of a stand-up comedian understands its relationship with the comedian. It is to connect or identify the implications of the comedian's jokes (whether self-deprecated or directed at the audience), which make the audience laugh. If the audience cannot connect the humor and perform the function of laughing, it loses interest in the comedian, and the confidence of the comedian, whose professional life depends on the laughs, becomes shattered. If boredom ensues, the comedian is booed off the stage. By contrast, the relationship between the audience and the playwright's monologue is slightly different. Even if the monologue is comedic, it has a dramatic focus which theater audience wishes to be engaged by. Finding that focus and the significance of the monologue requires the audience's full attention. As such, the frequent raucous laughter expected in a stand-up comedy would be disruptive to the audience's effort to have a total experience of the monologue.

More important, the theater audience is invested with the monologue, whose singular objective, beset by some conflict, anticipates some message or intention, which the audience is trying to figure out. This audience wants to know who or what raises the conflict with the speaker, that is, who or what causes the speaker to vaunt the monologue, and to what end. Unless he or she is a lunatic or in the habit of speaking to himself or herself (if so, this has to be made clear from the beginning) the speaker should be relating to something or somebody on stage. If the theater audience realizes it is also serving as the stage audience, it wants to know its identity, and under what circumstances it is serving. If it does not learn its identity, the theater audience may feel uncomfortable, like an innocent onlooker who is dragged into a family fight or an argument that the onlooker just happens to be observing. Theater audience in our modern convention has become a silent, polite observer that wishes to remain anonymous as far as possible—unlike, say, the groundlings of the Elizabethan stage whose participatory proclivity enjoyed being let into the innermost thoughts of troubled characters, such as Hamlet. If the modern audience is thus engaged, it becomes troubled and needs to know why it is being unnecessarily imposed upon.

The playwright may begin to resolve the problem of the monologue's "stage audience" by identifying the location of the incident or situation of the monologue. Let us create the character of Louise as the speaker of the monologue. If Louise is talking to herself, and is therefore her own "stage audience," the theater audience must understand, at once, whether she is a lunatic, whether the situation demands her speaking to herself, or whether she is known for talking out aloud. If not, the location may help motivate her monologue. By having Louise look around the room, the garden, the dungeon, the vehicle, in short the universe created for the monologue, the playwright might discover the impetus for the character to speak the very important first lines.

If, for instance, Louise is trying to confront the death of her husband, seeing a photograph of him in the bedroom or living room may spur her to speak and, therefore, to engage her objective action. If Louise contemplates seeking a divorce, her presence in the garden and the location of a rose bush may bring back memories of courtship. This may be the confirmation she needs to proceed with the divorce, or what makes her reconsider a plea to resolve the marital problem between her and her husband. But the location may provoke a comical action and monologue. Louise may be an absent-minded person who has misplaced her manicure-kit. Retracing her steps into the kitchen area could provide her with various distracting objects as she ransacks the utility closet—such as a pair of spectacles that had caused her to burn the turkey for Thanksgiving and forced her to buy a new pair.

A good example of a one-act monologue that grapples with and resolves satisfactorily the problem of the "stage audience" is *The Chemist*, by Roy Clarke[2]. The play is part of a collection of one-acts commissioned by the British television. However, because they were originally intended for television, most of the plays in the collection are not a very good example of a one-act monologue meant for the stage. With a television camera the director can engage the viewer's interest with visual insertions that compliment the present time of the monologue. As a stage play, the form that the published plays seem to suggest, most of the monologues remain simply a narrative of the past with nothing tangible happening at the present time of the plays. I will come back to this.

Vernon Duxley, the chemist and speaker of the monologue, sets a video camera in front of him; with this he wishes to document a marital agreement he had with his wife that morning before coming to work. Because he uses the video camera as a virtual interacting agent by which his monologue and objective-action become communicated or dramatized to the theater audience, the video camera is his "stage audience." In order to establish himself as the master of his domain, Vernon engages an objective-action of calling his wife at home to confirm their agreement. However, through the artful creative process of the playwright, the various obstacles Vernon encounters while thus engaged reveal him ironically and comically as an inadequate and failed husband—he not only cannot control his wife's extra-marital affairs, his display of macho-prowess is mere bark than bite.

The problem of the audience of a monologue is an important factor; resolving it helps the playwright distinguish between the "stage audience" and the theater audience. Bernard Grebanier, relating to the important question of the theater audience, reminds us, "No audience, no theater."[3] I would like to extend that statement to accommodate the "stage audience"—without a "stage audience," which here implies the character(s) who listen to and interact with the concerns of the central character on stage, there is no drama. In a one-act monologue, the "stage audience" is that virtual other or vehicle through which the drama is conveyed and the identity and objective of its one-character are realistically focused. For the playwright of a one-act monologue, determining that other for his or her stage is a challenge that is difficult, but rewarding when overcome.

THE SPEAKER

It should go without saying that the speaker, the voice of the monologue, needs an identity. But, again, beginners often take that identity for granted. Understanding why the voice needs to be characterized should help the playwright acknowledge the importance of character identity in general.

Let us go back to the image of the dramatist as singer. The note-idea that strikes the psyche of the singer/dramatist is transmitted to the deep recesses of the abdomen in the region of the diaphragm, from where it wells up the trachea to the larynx or voice-box, and comes out through the vibrating vocal-chords first as vocalized monotone. For the singer, the voiced monotone is often synchronous with the identity of the singer—unless it is in an operatic or dramatic mode. For a playwright, the voice of the monotonic expression requires an identity other than the playwright's. However, as implied, the character-identity that the playwright proposes is only an illusion, since in reality, or technically, the voice is the playwright's, and the identity (although a result of experience-encounters) accords with one or more of his many traits. Not unlike the voice of the singer, or an actor's for that matter, that assumes different characters.

In fact, the illusion of the identity speaks very much to the fact of realism. Realism (something, not real but like real) demands a different voice which, in reality, is the artist's or, in this case, the playwright's. On the other hand, although in reality the character's voice emanates from the playwright and is therefore the playwright's voice, still the voice must appear to be the voice of another, an illusion of identity. The situation is similar to that of an actor, whose identity hides under the character he or she is projecting. It is behind this illusory mask that the actor is able to project truthfully, that is, with the sincerity required to project the character. We must bear in mind that an actor projects a character interpretively; another actor may project it differently.

Thus, without going into the ramifications of the actor and verisimilitude, the experience of the actor's illusory mask is similar to the playwright's illusory voice, Louise for example, the voice needed to monologuize or dramatize the idea that struck. Paralleling these experiences is not as far fetched as we may think, that is, if we understand the fact that both are projectors of an art form, an illusion of reality. More important, the playwright's art precedes that of the actor who, as interpreter, is only taking the cue from the playwright, the originator of the voice. In an interesting way, this observation reveals the complex nature of the actor's art.

THE LOCATION

Where is Louise, the speaker/character of the monologue, located? Such a location also implicates the situation she is in. She is in such and such location because of such and such situation. Even if a playwright cannot at first determine the location clearly in terms of what constitutes it, and even if he or she is likely to change it, the playwright needs a location for the character to inhabit, to better serve the character and eventually the actor who plays the character. If we question the validity of a location's importance to the character, we only need to think of the word, habit, "clothing, apparel . . . a costume indicative or characteristic of a calling, rank, or function," and its possible associations with character.[4] The habit worn to clothe a character, apart from its cosmetic value, has many uses for the character—it shields from cold, from heat, provide protection over many health issues; more important, it helps define, somewhat, the character of its person—hence, the implications of a statement such as, "the character is like a habit worn" or, "the character fits him, like a glove." The "habit," the location or premises that a character inhabits, like a "habit" (character) worn, should ultimately help define the character's nature and actions. For what the location constitutes (objects, colors, shapes, etc.), surely, influences the preferences and sensitivities of the character that lives in it.

This in fact recalls the naturalist or positivist concept that the environment determines the character, as exemplified in plays by playwrights such as Henrick Ibsen. But the obverse is equally true—that the character determines the environment, in the sense that the character made the choice of the environment/location because of certain characteristics or limitations that identify the character. Vladimir, in one of his philosophical observations in Beckett's *Waiting for Godot*, indicates, "habit is a great deadener."[5] Although his conclusion is motivated by considerations of life and death, to which the act of waiting seems to have hopelessly compelled him and Estragon, we may realize that it is the "habit," the character worn as tramps, that has "deadened" them (indeed humankind) to their ritual routine of existence—waiting for some one in that location of survival (an isolated landscape where existence is doubtful, although fleetingly not impossible).

Indeed, it should be an intuitive response for any writer, especially of plays, to localize the arena of his or her ritual expression. Again, some beginners take locale for granted. They are struck by an idea and immediately embark on dialogue, only to discover the play is going nowhere and that the speakers and their dialogue lack specific character. In fact, the oversight may betray certain truths about the writer and a human failing of our television age—the fact that our critical perception has been dulled through being indulged. We often observe without necessarily seeing, or often see without necessarily observing. For instance, we can look at a façade of a building without necessarily taking into consideration the architectural reliefs or designs that constitute that façade. In terms of playwriting, it is easy for the novice playwright to take for granted that a theatrical set or a space is a technical appendage such that would be provided, in the main, by the production staff, headed by the director. Such an oversight ignores its importance as a protective structure, without which the character or characters may not be able to exist. Although the advice may seem unnecessary, given the exposures to theater or television, it is often wise to alert the student of the important possibilities of the stage space to a character.

In *The Chemist*, the office of Vernon Duxley, at the back of the main store, is a significant ritual arena for the character. For Vernon, it is a comfortable "habit" where order and authority still reside and his manhood is not threatened, at least not directly—unlike in the house he lives. He instructs his nondescript assistant in the main store that he doesn't want to be disturbed, and consequently sets his video camera, ready to document a conciliatory pact he made at home with his errant wife. At his office location, Vernon is the master of his domain, or so he thinks and boasts, or tries to convince himself with his macho exercises. When he realizes his wife's sexual aberrance is very much alive and enduring, he allows his vocational power over drugs to take possession of him—he considers concocting a humiliating potion for both his victims, a threat which however he is unable to carry out. Ultimately, it is a location that serves the playwright well to reveal Vernon's insecurity and fragile machismo.

The stage should be acknowledged by the playwright as a physical space that can be put to use in various ways, although such ways may not appear very visible to the playwright at first. Jacques, in that celebrated, rather inverted, chiasmic explication in Shakespeare's *As you Like It*, lets us, albeit indirectly, into its immense dimension (Act 2, scene 7, lines 139–166).[6] For the stage is a microcosmic world, full of microcosmic possibilities within the world's macrocosmic locations—the various options and circumstances by which the "players" (the multitudinous "seven ages" of man and their compounded coordinates of race, gender, upbringing, etc) situate their various characters, and make "their entrances and their exits."

Take another specific stage location as an example. Oedipus' palace, the physical world of Oedipus contained within the panoramic expanse of Athens' landscape, reflects the majestic authority of Oedipus.[7] The action he takes from moment to moment constitutes the choices his particular character makes, out of the many possibilities open to him, as he journeys through the limited time-span of his drama. Having demonstrated himself in the past as a riddle solver, he commands respect with his capable authority regarding the riddle that plagues his city and space of authority, a riddle that relates to the death of the previous king. However, that space, his authoritative world, is overshadowed by the fateful/fatal premonitions of the Olympian cosmos that seems to challenge his potential as a riddle solver. It is against this macrocosmic world of fate that Oedipus struggles adamantly, and through which we perceive his egotistic character, his hubris.

The fixed location of Greek theatrical convention, within which the different identities of its central characters situate or define themselves, obviously lends itself to numerous interpretations depending on its application. In the *Orestiea* of Aeschylus, for example, it serves as outside the royal palace in Argos, as Apollo's sanctuary in Delphi, then as the temple of Pallas Athena and the council hall of the Areopagus, both on the Acropolis[8]. Furthermore, these interpretive constructs have not only been realized within the permanent features of classical Greek stage, they have been conceived within the more flexible features of other theatrical conventions. They have also influenced the socio-political attitudes such that motivate the modern adaptations of the Greek plays, such as Jean Paul Sartre's *The Flies*, Eugene O'Neill's *Mourning Becomes Electra*, or Wole Soyinka's *The Bacchae of Euripides*. These location features (and ultimately these would include the costumes) whether for classical or for modern playwright, define the characters that inhabit the location; they are the characteristic "habit" worn by the characters, especially the central characters, that dwell in them. They are not there simply to dress the stage, as some might think, rather, they are there to be used variously in any way characteristic to or befitting each character. Without a good idea of how the features function within the location, characters that use or respond to them may not completely manifest to the playwright. Consequently, actors confronted with the roles created by the playwright may not be able to find the characters in order to embody and interpret them.

It is possible to argue, of course, that in classical plays such as Sophocles' *Oedipus* or Shakespeare's *Othello*, the playwright has not necessarily named specific locations, that some of the locations found in texts are editorial inserts. But several factors should be taken into account. Locations in these classical plays are often suggested by dialogue. A combination of these expressed clues and the researched theatrical conventions of the period often elicit the physical location of the particular play, along with its costumes, properties, gestures, etc.

Contrarily, it can be argued that the world view of these classical plays is somewhat unfamiliar to our present modern sensibilities, and that verifications of their conventions, the nature of which has been lost, are only configured by suppositions of exhaustive historical research. Against such an argument one should point out that, although the classical playwright may not have indicated locations or directions, coordinating producers or directors, which often included the playwright, knew the setting the playwright wanted and, consequently, informed the visual understanding of the audience through the playwright's choices, within the play, of scenic features and the accouterments of the characters that inhabit the locations.

At any rate, we must remember that in the classical periods (Greek, Roman, Medieval, and to a certain extent Elizabethan), the playwright's values, moralistic or political, were still in communal, synchronic bind with those of the audience. As such, it was possible to leave certain details to the assumption of the audience. By contrast in our modern world, such communal and intact values have become devalued, segmented, or mutated—through gradual manifestations of various historical (social, political, economic) developments such as the various revolutions and world wars. These conditions, in spite of the syncretic contraction of values among various cultures, evidently describe the complexity of the multifaceted, multi-cultured audience constituting our present theatrical convention. As such, it has become necessary for the playwright to be more specific, unless the playwright wishes his or her play to be misinterpreted. Numerous stories of production conflicts abound, between the playwright, who had a certain notion of what he or she has written, and therefore his or her director who regarded himself or herself as the artist of the theater and the director's vision more important than what the playwright was capable of expressing. Such conflicts often arise from a vaguely situated or not well focused play.

Actually, regarding these conflicts, some amelioration between these two artists is possible. A production as a theatrical enterprise requires the collaboration of the playwright (especially if he is around) and the director. Artistic egos aside, the playwright should be tolerant to the supposedly objective insight of an experienced director, whose creative vision should often validate as well as enrich that of the playwright. It should be recognized that even an inspired vision of a playwright may often have its boundaries, beyond which may require another vision to pierce through. On the other hand, the director should also respect the specific impulses in the playwright's psyche that gave expression to the playwright's vision, impulses which the director should make effort to understand. I shall come back to this.

With regard to location and the monologue, one of the things that the playwright should do, in order to avoid possible conflicts, is to perceive the location within which his or her character can function, a location that should help the playwright focus his or her character's objective. For instance, does Louise's emotional monotone emanate from her living room, her bedroom, or a funeral parlor? These different locations compel different motivations and situations. If Louise is in the bedroom, what items in the room might motivate Louise to speak her monologue—a pillow, a photograph on a night stand, the ceiling fan her husband had installed to make her more comfortable? And what is her objective-action as she emotes a recollection? Is she trying to come to terms with her husband's death? Is she getting up to go and pay an overdue utility bill which, if her fastidious husband were alive, would have been paid long before the due date?

Such questions can be asked, variously, with other locations. If it is a funeral parlor, is Louise by the coffin, fussing about the way her husband's body has been prepared? Is she waiting to talk to the funeral director in his office when she is arrested by the sight of a bouquet of flowers her husband disliked being brought into the chapel? While waiting, what is she doing to pass the time? Do memories of her husband remind her of something more comical? In fact, her actions might be comical—trying to remove a minute stain on the coffin to no avail, or to fix the spectacles that slipped down the nose of her husband's corpse. As these images occur, countless associations and suppositions would strike the psyche of the playwright, especially if the playwright poses relevant questions. Here, that common adage becomes applicable—heaven helps those who help themselves. The creative psyche, if prodded, is capable of generating astonishing possibilities.

PRESENT TIME

Asking questions can also bring into focus the dramatized present time of the play. This time is seemingly concurrent with the present time of the theater audience, making the actor live it afresh and the audience experience it as live. As stated, this realistic and important moment, unfortunately, is often overlooked and not realized in the monologue, because the monologue is mistakenly thought to simply recall the past. But really, no play engages its audience in the past, or better still, no playwright can engage an audience with past events without relating that past to present circumstances. Even in story telling, especially in the traditional setup, this principle applies. It is what the storyteller does while telling the story, usually about a past event, that makes the audience listen. For the story to be engaging, the past points to a moral or a message, which implicates a present circumstance. But more than this, the storyteller involves the audience in the present by singing, dancing, making jokes—diverting the boredom of relating the past with something of the moment. By so doing, the storyteller creates some suspense from the moral or the message of the story. In this regard, a reading from a novel by the writer often fails to engage its audience, unless the writer radiates a charisma that is attractive. Even so, if the reading went for too long, it might become less engaging or boring—because the writer-reader had nothing much more to engage the audience's visual attention, except standing at the podium to read. Understanding this problem, some writers would cracks jokes here and there during the reading; others rely on their interpretive and performance abilities. All these are skills or activities in the present time of the reading that could engage the audience in the story being told.

The monologue as a dramatized story challenges the writer's creativity in the task of realizing the present, and in lifting it from the sphere of storytelling, a narration of past events. In reality, the "story" being told in a one-act dramatic monologue, indeed in any form of drama, only complements what is happening at the present time of the play. It is the past circumstance that makes the present circumstance understood more clearly, and functions in a similar way that the dialogue does to the visual enactment—complements present action. We would love to hear what Louise has to say about her dead husband, but in order for her to engage us in the story, she would have to be doing something, relevant to the story, at the present time of her narrative or presentation. She would have to be involved in a present action that is caused by an objective, an action that is consequential and gravitates to some climax and denouement. In other words, the monologue has to have a plot.

Let us illustrate the fact further with the example of *The Chemist* and its character, Vernon Duxley. While Vernon is telling us how he made up with his wife after her affair with his supposed friend Greg Stiles, he is in the present time of the play, in front of the theater audience, trying to reassert himself (really, he is affirming his manhood) as master of the house. First he checks on his wife—trying unsuccessfully to call her at home, in the guise of reaffirming their agreement. Then, he engages himself in exercises (push-ups, weigh-lifts, etc) that, he hopes, would help maintain or prove his sexual prowess. Thus we, the audience, are faced with the ultimate question: Will he in reality be able to assert himself as the master of the house? That question becomes more persistent when Vernon calls Greg's house and discovers is wife is there with Greg—obviously his wife has not changed her aberrant behavior. Vernon then, in a final effort of his objective, considers using his chemical expertise to devise a drug that would make his wife grow a beard, and transform his licentious friend into a monster. For this seems the only way he could become the master of his domain. However, his aborting of the plan at the climax, perhaps realizing the criminal consequences of the act or the grotesque implications on his relationship, means he will not be able to assert himself.

A one-act dramatic monologue does not simply tell a story, it functions as a play. This means it has all the ingredients of a play—character, that character's objective and the action the objective describes in stages at the present time of the monologue. This action, with its conflict develops to a climax and then resolves itself.[9] Confronting and overcoming the challenges of a one-act monologue should make the problems of playwriting as a whole easier to define and deal with. For a normal one-act and a full-length are only dramatic extensions of the monologue, which evolves as a monotone, that is, before it develops its colors and ritual impulses as a monologue, a normal one-act or a full-length.

NOTES

1. Shakespeare, *Hamlet, Prince of Denmark* (Cambridge: Cambridge University Press, 1985), 145–48; 88–90.

2. Roy Clarke, "The Chemist" in *Single Voices: The Book of the TV Series* (London: BBC Books, 1990), 15–28.

3. Bernard Grebanier, *Playwriting: How to Write for the Theater* (New York: Harper & Row, 1961), 1–2.

4. Gove, Philip B., ed. *Webster's Third New International Dictionary*, unabridged (MA: Merriam-Webster, Inc., 1986), 1017.

5. *Waiting for Godot*, 58.

6. The Arden Shakespeare, *As You Like It*, ed Agnes Latham (London: Methuen & Co., 1975), 55–57.

7. For a concise description of this landscape, see Stanley L. Glenn *The Complete Actor* (Boston: Allyn and Bacon, Inc., 1977), 168–181.

8. See *The Orestes Plays of Aeschylus*, translated by Paul Roche (New York: Penguin-Mentor, 1962).

9. See Appendix II for an example of a complete monologue.

Chapter Six

Ritual Scope and Developments: *The One-Act and the Full-Length*

The one-act monologue is useful exercise that challenges the skills of the playwright, the skills needed for writing a regular one-act and a full-length play. To be able to meet the demands that the monologue poses is to anticipate or mastermind the questions that any play raises in the creative psyche when the idea-note manifests itself for a dramatic development.

To reiterate the fact of the creative process, a creative/dramatic development for the theater is a ritual process that begins with the playwright, whose psyche is struck with an idea-note potent with associational and consequential (dramatic) possibilities. This idea-note becomes emoted or expressed through a ritual confrontation and struggle, which structures the raw material into a dramatic form, constituting character(s), visual substance, conflict and dialogue. In the process, the playwright is at one with his or her central focus (character or idea), through whom or which the playwright must ritualize an objective need that must be pursued, and resolved one way or another. It is by no means an easy process, and the expression is neither automatic, nor guaranteed. Both the idea and its subsequent expression must be nurtured through rigorous investigative inquiry (psychical and physical) and persistent modifications, before a satisfactory realization of the drama is achieved.

The potent possibilities for a dramatic expression could be single or multi directional. In other words, the idea could be given a monotonal rendering, or be conceived for many voices. In fact, the process almost always begins with a monotonic-monologic register, which will then develop in a simple or complex expression of the situation of things, such that determines a one-act or a full-length. Furthermore, the expression could be emoted as an abstract idea-development within a de-emphasized action (such as in *Waiting for Godot*), or as an objective-action of an abstract idea (as in *Oedipus Rex*). It could also express characteristics of some form of seriousness or some form of ridicule, or both. In fact, given the creative, versatile disposition of the playwright, or the inventive limitations of the idea, the expression could be a combination of any of these possibilities. Simply put, the potential of writing a play, when the idea strikes in the creative psyche, is diverse, but the expression of any of its possibilities follow a similar ritual process of emoting. However, differences in expression may also lie in versatility of the questing mind, the types of questions imposed on the psyche to stimulate a dramatic expression. This chapter will extend the scope of the one-act monologue to its possible development of a regular one-act and a full-length, thereby showing the versatile ritual connection among these forms.

As established, the given circumstances of a monologue are mostly narrated. But since given circumstances, like in all plays, have to realize an action in the present time of the play, (usually through some crisis), the narration of the monologue should be focused with an incident that develops the play's moment. Such an incident will be initiated through an objective of the monologue's single character; in a regular one-act or a full-length, that incident will be generated through the interacting objectives of multiple characters. It all depends on the kind of quest the playwright imposes on his central character.

In *The Chemist*, Roy Clarke, the playwright, confronts the challenge to emote the idea-note that struck for a single voice. Actually, considering the fact that the initial register of the note is singular and monotonic, the challenge is not so much extending the monotone into the singular utterance of the monologue (although this applies), as making that utterance dramatic and engaging. For instance, if the idea-note of *The Chemist* is "reconciliation," the playwright chooses Vernon Duxley as central and single character of the utterance. Thus, anticipating the dramatic problems of simply extending the given circumstances (an extension of the idea-note) the playwright invents a motivating device for his character to help him narrate the given circumstances and initially engage the theater audience—this is the video camera that serves as a "stage audience." But he also needs to sustain the engagement of theater audience through the life of the monologue

The given circumstances generated from the idea-note express the marital reconciliation and understanding that Vernon Duxley established with his wife the past weekend, which was intended to put an end to his wife's extramarital sexual diversion. This immediate circumstance has a narrative history that the character needs to document—directly to the "stage audience," and indirectly to the theater audience. In order to engage the theater audience dramatically through the life of the narration, the playwright needs to focus these given circumstances with an objective-action in the present time of narration.

He asks questions such as, "What does Vernon want?" "Why does he want it?" "What is he doing towards getting what he wants?" Thus, Vernon's preoccupation or objective, his attempt to document, begins to assume a macho attitude. Vernon's endeavors or strategies of realizing his objective (recording the past, attempting to reach his wife by phone, working off his frustrations with physical exercises) are really attempts to regain his much humiliated manhood. This overall preoccupation becomes the central action of the play. We realize that Vernon's narration and action are more a battle with himself than with his wife, a condition that can, with some art of economy, be contained within a one-act monologue.

However, the playwright could develop the monologue, along with its given circumstances and singular objective, into a regular one-act or, perhaps, a full-length. Such an option gives the playwright an advantage of involving other characters; but then, this would involve other issues and questions. The situation may remain the same—a man trying to reaffirm or legitimize his marital authority as the master of the house, or a man trying to reestablish his shattered manhood. If he is the central character, so may remain his central objective, although, perhaps not quite as singular. In the objective of the monologue, the man is trying to reaffirm or legitimize his authority as husband for himself. In the regular one-act, he may be establishing that authority in the presence of his wife, or of the person who is the subject of his wife's adultery, Greg Stiles—in the monologue both are absent. Vernon may also establish his position for both wife and Greg, for instance, where he probably has successfully trapped them.

The modification means Vernon's objective would include his wife, Marlene, or Greg, or both. For example, Vernon's objective may be modified thus: To prove to his wife that he is the master of the house. We are familiar with dramas that focus such a macho objective, whether on stage or television. For instance, Willy Loman in *Death of a Salesman* gives us a more complex dimension of this preoccupation. If Vernon's attempt to prove his masculinity is for both Marlene and Greg, the objective may be expressed thus: To prove to the offending fornicators, or adulterers, that he is the master of his house. You may note that this objective, like that of the monologue has a ring of the comedic to it, especially if he is trying to trap, or has successfully trapped both characters—although deciding whether the play is going to be a comedy, tragedy or otherwise should not be the priority of the writer at this stage. However, either objective will modify not only the situation, but also the singular action of the monologue. The possibilities are limitless, but first let us acknowledge the new ritual attitude to given circumstances.

In a regular one-act, or any play with more than one character, given circumstances do not have to be narrated, although some of it could, given the uncommon style of plays such as Tennessee Williams' *The Glass Menagerie*—where we have the narrator as the central character introducing the past in flash-backs, which he is using to justify his present action[1]. Rather, given circumstances are more often dramatized in dialogue and action. This means that, one way or another, the two or multiple characters that the playwright anticipates for the one-act will implicate or reference the circumstances—not in one stretch, but at various moments throughout the play.

Say the given circumstances of the one-act monologue are still operative, and Vernon objective is to prove to Marlene he is still the master of the house, the regular one-act's situation could modify into the fact of Vernon trying to confine Marlene to the house. The question that now faces the playwright is: How does Vernon go about doing this? In other words, what ways or actions (really, strategies) would he use to confine slippery Marlene to the house? These strategies are the specific devices the playwright invents for Vernon to define the central action of confining Marlene. The kind of strategies summoned up for Vernon, of course, would greatly depend on the kind of person Marlene is, and her art of slipperiness. The question is whether Vernon is going to be successful or not with these strategies, question the playwright should ask but may not be able to answer or assess just yet—certainly not before he or she has put Vernon to the test, or to the challenge Marlene poses.

Perhaps Vernon's central objective is to try and get her locked up in the bedroom. First, as he shows off with his macho-exercises, he wants her to help him pick up a new towel in the bedroom closet. But he meets with opposition—Marlene is reluctant because she seems to have another agenda, suggested by the spasmodic concentration she poses on her manicure and fingernail painting. This preoccupation with fingernails has put Vernon on the alert in the first place. Perhaps Vernon then storms into the bedroom, only to come back to raise a row about the still unmade bed—Marlene should have made it since she was the last to get up. However, Marlene is in no hurry to do that job either, more especially because of her preoccupation; in fact, she asks her "darling" Vernon to help her do it. Yet when the phone rings, she jumps at it. Vernon registers this attitude and becomes hopeful with his objective—if the call is from Greg, Marlene would want to have the phone conversation in private, and therefore would probably walk into the bedroom. If she does, would Vernon finally be able to achieve his objective of locking her in? For his achievement may be complicated by a host of other factors—for instance, Marlene may lock the door herself and take the key with her, or her phone conversation may be so secretly short, or she may not even go to the bedroom. The playwright should be open to these possibilities to dramatize the right choice.

Every obstacle shows and tests the inventive capacity of the playwright, which in turn could make the play very engaging and entertaining. Incidentally, the playwright's choice of central focus might change for the new one-act. It could be Marlene who had a more crucial objective—she needs to go and meet her lover; therefore, she is biding time to let Vernon go to the office. Such an objective would also change the situation. Also, if the playwright has aspirations for a full-length, he has the advantage of dramatizing the given circumstances more fully, by extending the present situation to contain two or more incidents that are separated by passage of time and, perhaps, have multiple locations. The main objective may remain the same, or modify to include Greg.

These examples should help illustrate the point, even if they tend to be oversimplification. Important changes to note are modifications of singularity in terms of situation and action. In a one-act with two or more characters, the potential for a dialogic exchange breaks up the monotonic singularity of a one-act monologue thereby modifying situation and action. However, the limitations of space and time of a monologue also often applies in a regular one-act. Both forms function well in a single location and in a continuous moment of time; but the location, as might be assumed, is not necessarily confined to structured areas of a building such as an office, a living room or a bedroom. To violate the limitations by indulging in multiple locations and time of events, as sometimes found in some one-acts, is to encroach the province and latitude of a full-length play. Unless the one-act is a play of ideas, that is, dramatizing an idea that develops in stages, multiple scenes that evolve through an objective action may stand out as underdeveloped incidents or acts of a full-length play.[2]

Because of its limitations, any one-act challenges the inventive power of the playwright. Good examples of such imaginative one-acts abound—such as Edward Albee's *Zoo Story* and Sam Shepard's *Fool for Love*, discussed initially in chapter two. Both plays observe the limitations of a one-act, and both playwrights have taken advantage of the challenges the one-act limitations imposed on their creative sensibilities. Also, the given circumstances of these regular one-acts are more dramatized than narrated, and in both plays the single location and the continuous moment test the resourcefulness of the writers. Furthermore, the singularity that could have occurred with any of the characters to produce a one-act monologue is now shared. Or, to be more specific, the singularity of the central character is shattered, obstructed and challenged by the presence of two or more characters, making it easier for the playwrights to explore and resolve the constraints of a one-act. Let us now relate more fully to the given circumstances and the dramatized present action of the plays before determining their potential for the more restrictive one-act monologue, or the scope of their possible development to a full-length.

In *A Fool for Love*, Eddie and May had an innocent incestuous relationship brought about, some time in the past, by the clandestine extramarital relationship their father had with May's mother. Through the traumas of the relationships (extramarital and incestuous), May's mother had been beside herself and Eddie's mother had, apparently, shot herself dead—facts known to both May and Eddie but in various versions of acknowledgment. The father, the parent connection for both Eddie and May, had died before the present action of the play. Since their relationship became known to them as illicit, May and Eddie have been in a kind of emotional struggle and dilemma—trying to coming to terms with a love that binds them and the parental/societal values that oppose their relationship. They have made several attempts to break apart, to no avail.

In a one-act monologue, either Eddie or May as its single character could narrate these given circumstances although differently, according to the way each knows and is impacted by the circumstances. The challenge of such a monologue would be to find a present time of the monologue, and a situation with a potential for dramatic motivation. This motivation would serve, within the monologue's location, as a "stage audience," the virtual character to whom or which the narrator emotes the past, and with whom or which that narrator interacts dramatically in the present time—in a way that is not obtrusive or contrived, but realistic. As stated, the theater audience could be that "stage audience" if the writer of the monologue and his or her character is explicit about the role of the theater audience, that is whom it represents. However, we must bear in mind that such a monologue would be a different play by a different author, for it is not the option that the creative process of the Sam Shepard has taken. The playwright, for reasons best known to the dynamics of his creative psyche, has chosen the regular one-act form, which of course also has it limitations and challenges. Let us look at the situation and present action in Shepard's play.

The present time of *A Fool for Love* dramatizes the struggle between Eddie and May. They have come together again, only to resist each other's intimacy with jealous suspicions. May thinks Eddie has a lover of a Countess, a fact that Eddie denies; Eddie's masculinity is challenged almost with impotency at the thought that May has a lover whose presence is imminent. The possibility of either condition repels as well as binds. But to really focus this present time and the action it describes, we will have to relate to the central character and his or her objective.

As established, the central character could be either character, although the objective-action would be different in either case. With Eddie, who has returned to May, his objective is to try and make the relationship binding this time around, probably with the idea of staying with May permanently—although that possibly is ultimately debatable. But the objective focuses his strategies, which include reassuring May by denying the existence of the

Countess, and using cowboy macho tactics (cleaning a gun, and swirling a lasso) to affirm his position. If the central character is May, who has been fleeing from one location to another to avoid Eddie, although leaving enough tracks as to her whereabouts, her objective is to resist Eddie so that she could go on with her life. She tries to do this in many ways—rejecting him outright through her persistent awareness of the Countess (her smell, her image, etc.), and then by expressing expectations of a lover, Martin, who eventually appears. Another objective, actually for either character, might be to challenge the legitimacy of their relationship with the view to making a definitive decision.

One of the ways Shepard dramatizes the given circumstances is evoking the physical presence of the father, not only as a link between the two characters but also between the past and the present. In a way, going by what we established earlier, the presence of the figure seems to demonstrate a connection between the *illud tempus*, which a playwright broaches with a creative idea, and its manifested presence as a stage text. Without the *illud tempus*-figure and its/his revelations, the playwright's objective to ritualize his expression of the idea that struck cannot become validated or understood. Seen by the theater audience, the figure/character is an evocation of what both May and Eddie conceive of it/him, or what the playwright perceives and realizes for his characters. Consequently, the playwright dramatizes the different perception of each character of their father, especially in relation to their separate mothers. It would be interesting to see how the figure, as a motivating agent of the present, would have played out in a one-act monologue—with either Eddie or May as the monologue's single and singular character.

The objective of either character raises a question of achievement with regard to their bonding. With Eddie: Will he be able to make the relationship binding? With May: Will she be able to resist Eddie once and for all? Or, perhaps, with either one: Will he or she be able to make a definitive decision in terms of their relationship? For each, the question should be answered at the climax. In resolving either question, Shepard demonstrates his power of invention that might have eluded the inexperience of a budding one-act playwright.

Shepard's important dramatic device is the father—with him the playwright is able to sustain the one-act without any interruption, and to pose an opposition to both main characters' perception of their relationship, principally Eddie's. By wishing to make the relationship binding, Eddie confronts a stiff but subtle opposition of the father. As the Old Man suggests, the opposite perceptions taken by him and his son raise questions of realism and reality.[3] May's objective of resisting the relationship also encounters an opposition from the father. Her confused mind and resistance, apart from being fostered by the illicit nature of the relationship, probably grew out of knowing the way her mother had suffered (going berserk from the hopeless love of the father), the way the mother begged her to abort her relationship with Eddie, and, perhaps more significant, the way Eddie's mother "blew her brains out" through her knowledge of Eddie's intimacy with May[4]. Judging by his concept of love (at best illusory) the Old Man would not allow himself to see the tragic implications that derived from his sexual perversion; he consequently denies May's recall of her mother's suffering and Eddie's mother's ultimate response.

Both oppositions from the father are, conversely, met with relative resistance, making Eddie and May seek each other's support, if only for a moment. As the Old Man pleads for Eddie's support in male bonding, Eddie and May pull to an embrace, and it looks as if their relationship would be binding after all.[5] However, the climax shatters that notion for us. Shepard gives a specific direction: *"Headlights suddenly arc across the stage . . . cutting across the stage through window. . . . Sound of loud collision, shattering glass, an explosion . . . "*[6] The intrusion of the outside force of light and sound, exposes and shatters any hope of their bonding.

In spite of the conclusion we make of the significance of light and sound, the analysis of *Fool for Love* is a straightforward reading of the play, in terms of the creative process of the playwright within a normal one-act expression. It has not attempted to impose any psychological, symbolic interpretation the play may provoke.

In *Zoo Story*, we encounter another example of the playwright's creative process expressing itself in the regular one-act form. Here as in *A Fool for Love*, the playwright, with equal inventiveness and economy, mostly dramatizes the given circumstances between the play's two characters, as opposed to narrating them with one of the characters. But here, there is no ambiguity as to who the central character is; therefore we can say that this character, in contrast to his possible rendition of a monologue, most of the time dramatizes the given circumstances through dialogue and interaction with another character. Jerry, the central character, a kind of wanderer and foundling in the difficult existence of New York City, is tired of living in isolation. He has tried much of his life to connect with people and even with animals, but to no avail. Both his parents, whom he probably does not know, are presumed dead. Tired of his isolation, he wants to make a strong statement about it, even if it means ending his life. He has therefore gone to the zoo, perhaps as a last resort to understand his isolation or to make connections, or as an affirmation of his death wish. These are experiences or events expressed as given circumstances.

At the present time of the play, Jerry is returning from the zoo. He encounters another individual, Peter, who, by his appearance and preoccupation, seems also in isolation—a white-collar, he has gotten away from home chores and relationship to find a quiet spot on a park bench for his reading diversion. While Peter's assumed (superficial) isolation at first poses no visible opposition to Jerry's society-imposed (factual or existential) isolation, it begs to be challenged to a kind of duel of acknowledgment. In other words, Peter's appearance suggests him as a likely subject for Jerry's intended statement.

Jerry objective, therefore, is to challenge Peter's superficial isolation, in an effort to make Peter understand real isolations such as Jerry's, and perchance make Peter subsequently confront his own condition. In other words, Jerry's confrontational statement desperately wishes to comment on his isolation in such a way that forces Peter to acknowledge his, even if it spells danger or death for Jerry.

Jerry's strategies for his objective constitute the action of the plot. At first, he forces Peter to engage in a conversation with him, by accosting his sense of curiosity with, "I've been to the zoo." Securing Peter's attention, Jerry engages Peter with a story about his unsuccessful attempts to make connections, even with a dog. Thus unguarding Peter's defenses, Jerry forces Peter to defend his assumed isolation and space on the bench, by harassing him to the point of violence. Awakening Peter's sense of protest, Jerry offers Peter an implement of defense—a knife. However, realizing Peter's hopeless reluctance or failure to understand Jerry's desperate situation, let alone Peter's own fact of isolation, Jerry immolates himself on the knife Peter is holding. It is only at that time that Peter recognizes Jerry's agony and desperation, and what it feels like to be really isolated. Jerry, as he implies earlier, has taken a long but significant way to educate Peter about isolation.

Again, although we are not so much interested here in symbolisms and in the psychological interpretation of this play, as in the sequences of action that describes the singular objective of the central character, one factor is worth mentioning. It is a significant factor that suggests the playwright's power of invention, and which might implicate possible modifications from the regular one-act to a monologue or a full-length.

The playwright's choice of names would seem to suggest some glaring images. We have a feeling that the playwright intends us to make somewhat onomatopoeic associations with the names in order to ply a deeper perception of the play—Jerry resonating Jesus, and Peter recalling Jesus' disciple, the fisherman Peter.[7] In fact, we may note that the playwright forces us to make these parallels in the final scene of the play. Up till then, Peter has failed, or refused to acknowledge Jerry's isolation and need. Now with Jerry's impalement, when Peter finally gets it, he cries out: "Oh my God . . . Oh my God . . . Oh my God . . . " The response from Jerry signals the clue: "Thank you, Peter. I mean that, now . . . I came unto you . . . and you have comforted me. Dear

Peter."⁸ The biblical reference evokes the figure of the disciple Peter who, like the Albee's Peter has refused to acknowledge Jerry's isolation and need, denied Christ three times only to realize the implications of that denial later, thereby becoming the fisher of men. Presumably, Albee's Peter, being a journalist, would similarly bring the public to his newly acquired consciousness of people in isolation.

Both *A Fool for Love* and *Zoo Story* dramatize very well as regular one-act, one with four characters, and the other, two. Although the situation for each play emerges from a monotonic idea-note that has struck (let's say the idea-note is "Bonds of Love" for *A Fool for Love* and "Isolation" for *Zoo Story*), each playwright's creative choice might not eventually have favored a one-act monologue. However, with the given circumstances and present action of the plays in mind, let us see how possible it is to develop a monologic form for each of them.

In terms of our understanding of the process, it is possible to suggest that the story of the dog, perhaps, first engaged Albee's creative psyche, whether he was conscious of it or not. The narrative, apparently, is "the key element of Jerry's ritual" and, if I may add, of playwright Albee's ritualization of the idea-note that struck his psyche, about isolation.⁹ If so, Jerry has the potential of being the single character of a monologue, who narrates the story of the dog as well as the rest of the given circumstances. His objective might be similar to that in the regular one-act—to make people (the audience) aware of his isolation. It might also take a more singular form, to kill himself. However, the playwright needs to develop such an objective with a present-time action and, to avoid talking directly to the theater audience, with a "stage audience" or something that motivates Jerry's objective action and monologue. Perhaps the character comes to sit in the park, then brings out a knife or a gun from his pocket and struggles with himself why he should or should not kill himself. This somewhat recollects a monologue from Shakespeare, when Macbeth sees an implement that might serve his murderous purpose: "Is this a dagger I see before me . . . "(*The Tragedy of Macbeth* Act 2, sc. 1, lines: 34–65)¹⁰ Or, wanting to establish a biblical parallel, the playwright might suggest a phrase of a preacher, probably about Christ, quoted in the newspaper lying on the bench, which Jerry tries to come to terms with as he engages his monologue. Jerry's motivating agent could also be a cross-like structure that he finds in the park.

But the writer of the monologue might invent another location for the character, and another present time action consistent with the character's objective. Many possibilities may present themselves to help the playwright develop his or her monologue. Obviously, for Albee, a more effective choice is the dialogic form, in which the physical presence of another character, Peter, contrasts and plays off Jerry's impositions of his isolation.

The Old Man's narration in *A Fool for Love* might also have been first conceived by Shepard from the idea that struck.[11] The father narrates a rather surreal incident experienced by the family in a car "Plymouth I think it is," an encounter that poses terror to May. The creative psyche of Shepard might have tentatively considered the monologic form with Old Man as the single character, whose objective is to narrate a past that informs the present crisis of his children. If so, problems of present action and "stage audience" would have arisen. In trying to resolve these problems, the playwright might have attempted using the three characters (Old Man, Eddie and May) one at a time to narrate their own version of the story, given the present situation of the children, a result of the father's extramarital diversion. Possible "stage audience" and motivator for the present time action of the monologue might include the Plymouth or an automobile that evokes it, the invisible presence of the "Countess," the "portmanteau" May uses to move from one location to another, the saddle and lasso brought in by Eddie, etc. All these possible "stage audiences" which inform the regular one-act he finally wrote, might suggest an objective that engages the present time of the monologue.

To recap, the character emoting exercise—such as suggested for the Eddie, May and Old Man—has its creative value. It allows each character to bare his or her thoughts out, truthfully, without the fear of the presence and/or interference of another character. It is the ritual stage of the creative process, whether by psychical or physical exploration, when the playwright strives to locate a character that could best serve his or her creative needs. Once the playwright realizes the character and the most effective way to dramatize the character's objective, aligned with the playwright's own objective of writing a play, all the other possibilities become secondary although are still subject to being used. They become accessories that may or may not help to dramatize the conflict(s) that beleaguer the objective-action of the central character. Such a process of development may have resulted in Shepard's one act with the two main characters, along with two other characters helping the conflicting main characters to negotiate their drama.

As stated earlier, because of the situation that binds the two main characters, it is arguable that either could serve as the central character, although Eddie would seem to be the more feasible, by the fact of his re-intrusion into May's life and living. But either way, the other two characters serve as accessories to Eddie and May's conflict: the father as a force of the past and the link to the main characters' emotional crisis; Martin, as a force of the present that poses a threat to their bonds of love. Also evoked, as a counterbalance to Martin's internal threat, is the Countess—the external threat that develops as a kind of "happy idea."[12] This dramatic idea resonates through the play, becoming useful to the playwright at the play's climax when headlights from outside arc over, exposing Eddie and May's illicit, passionate embrace—lights presumed from the Countess' automobile. Thus, the exposure and subsequent collision and explosion—the probable existence of the Countess—shatters the likelihood of Eddie and May's projected bonding of love.

The ritual scope of both *The Zoo Story* and *A Fool for Love* is limited to the dialogic one-act form. We have raised and explored the possibility of restricting that scope further to a monologic form. But is there a possibility of extending the scope to a full-length? In terms of duration of time, both one-acts in fact possess a length close to that usually expected of a full-length play. Therefore, it seems the possibility of evolving a full-length would be only a matter of preference—except that length is the least determinant of that form.

To be sure, the ritual scope of a full-length is wider, in contrast to the restricting tightness of a one-act. However that latitude, although much more complex in ritual engagement, has dramatic resources capable of encompassing intervals of time and of situating themselves in various locations. Any of Shakespeare's plays elaborately demonstrates dramatic complexity of a full-length—with its multiple incidents, locations, characters and plots, all connected by a central ritual focus. In some of our contemporary, commercial efforts, disregarding the musicals, that complexity has gradually become controlled by the production budget that often prefers to account for one location, and a few characters.

Given the intricate scope of a full-length, an important factor to consider regarding the possibility of extending *A Fool for Love* and *Zoo Story* is whether the tight action of each one-act could be broken up, or stretched to accommodate the dramatic resources of a full-length. In one respect, the attempt is tantamount to challenging the psychic integrity of the writer of either play that has chosen the limited scope of the one-act in the first place. For the result of the attempt is bound to realize a different play. However, in order to explore the possibility, we would have to relate to three ritual elements of the one-acts—the situation, the objective-action of the central character, and the scope of the theme, that is, the idea of the play as conceived in the creative psyche of the playwright.

SITUATION

A major difference between a one-act and a full-length is the extension of the ritual scope from a restrictive limited, to a wider, more inclusive realization. This difference in scope, usually attributed to the number of acts, can be understood by making clear the distinction between a situation and an incident, terms we often used interchangeably. We tend to suggest a one-act play as having only one situation. But so should any play have for that matter, even though the scope of a full-length is wider. The confusion reflects the loose meaning with which we render the word situation. First, let us consider the dictionary explanations of the two words. Situation: "the way in which something is placed in relation to its surroundings; a particular or striking complex of affairs at a stage in the action of a narrative or drama." Incident: "an occurrence of an action or situation that is a separate unit of experience."[13] Even by these Webster's Collegiate Dictionary meanings, we can immediately locate a slight distinction between the two terms—we may note that an incident is contained within a situation. Therefore, in terms of playwriting, we can be more confident to suggest that a one act has a situation with one incident, whereas a full-length has a situation with two or more incidents. It is these incidents that constitute the acts of a full-length.

The situation of *A Fool for Love* (with Eddie as the central character) is something like this: Eddie, having driven so many miles in search of May, comes back to her to try and make permanent their illicit relationship (or, to try and stabilize their illicit relationship). That situation may be too restrictive for a full-length, unless it incorporates other elements capable of extending its boundaries. For example: Eddie, wishing to relieve himself of the guilt of his illicit relationship with May, with the view to stabilizing the relationship, confronts the various demons that have haunted him for years. This new situation allows the exploration of other possible incidents contained within it, which may also make the father more functional. The play may explore a first incident or act that reveals Eddie's haunting problems with May and the way they affect other relationships, a second incident/act that confronts his father and his extra-marital relationship, a third incident/act that tries to resolve his crisis with May, for good or bad. As we can see, a play with an incident has been transformed to one with three incidents, although the incidents are linked with a consistent objective of Eddie—to be able to stabilize his relationship with May. However, this is far from the intentions of Shepard who, with economy, control, and inventiveness, has contained Eddie's objective within the tightness of a one-act.

Similarly we may try and extend the situational scope of *Zoo Story*. Its original situation can be expressed thus: Jerry, whose inability to make connections has isolated him, seeks to impact Peter with a statement about his isolation. To be able to flesh it out to a full-length, we would have to make that situation more inclusive. For example: Jerry, coming to terms with his isolation at the zoo, desperately seeks to make a statement of his isolation that would impact other lives (or the world). Such a situation may or may not include Peter; it may also be located at the zoo to include several people. With a single set, the situation could express incidents or acts that have different time intervals, which would make it possible for Jerry to confront various people with his objective of making a statement about his isolation. For Jerry may not have succeeded with one person, so that with each successive person or incident he becomes more desperate. Furthermore, the way he finally makes his statement, by killing himself, may be different from that in Albee's play. At any rate, some of these possibilities probably racked the psyche of Albee for consideration, that is, before he finally settled for the economical, more challenging and inventive form of the one-act. As such, we cannot but wonder at the disciplined craftsmanship of Albee's creative psyche in expressing the desperation of isolation within the limited scope of the play.

By contrast, the situational ritual scope of his *Who's Afraid of Virginia Woolf*, for instance, is much wider, one with a central character, George, whose objective, among invaders of his privacy, is to resist and challenge at every turn Martha's freewheeling of the secrets that constitute their marital relationship. In that play, the playwright demonstrates his capacity to dramatize an extensive scope with a different level of creative awareness, but with equal ingenuity as with his one-act.

OBJECTIVE ACTION

To recognize the distinction we have made, between a situation and an incident, is to begin to have an understanding of the objective-action that the restrictive situation (of a one-act), or the extensive situation (of a full-length) initiates. For the central character usually describes his or her objective within a given situation or incident. However, in extending the scope of *Zoo Story* and *A Fool for Love*, we may have observed that the main objective of the central character does not necessarily change. At best, it is modified. In other words, the objective increases its situational span from one incident to many, so that there are subsidiary objectives within the central objective.

As we have established, by extending the scope of a one-act to a full-length, the situation needs to accommodate, or at least suggest the accommodation of, two or more incidents. The objective-action does not necessarily change because it could easily extend the boundaries of a single incident (of a one-act) into the scope of multiple incidents (of a full-length). For example, while the objective-action of Eddie in *A Fool for Love* may be similar to that of its potential full-length, that is, to try and stabilize his forbidden relationship or bonds of love, that objective continues its action in subsequent incidents of the proposed full-length. However, each of the subsequent incidents may have its own sub-objective. In a similar fashion, the objective-action of

Zoo Story may not change significantly. In general, it impels Jerry to make an impactive statement of his isolation; but since the scope of a possible full-length is wider, that objective expresses itself in various sub-objectives within its multiple incidents.

However, the central character with any objective-action, whether in a one-act or a full-length, needs strategies for his or her action. The character wants to achieve something, but how does he or she go about achieving it? Because of the incidental nature of a one-act, these strategies often tend to be more sharply defined, for reasons that could be conjectured. For instance, the limited ritual scope of expression in a one-act demands urgency and conciseness. While the ritual/dramatic components are intact, they do not allow for gradual development of the characters, whose temperament, individuality and objective-action need to be established immediately. Furthermore, since the crisis that brings the central character into being needs resolving within a short time, it is almost like the character has no allowance for assessing the situation he or she is in. The character has to time to gather support or evidences, so to speak, before deciding on a possible action; neither does he or she have time for the subtleties of hesitation and delaying tactics. Oedipus, even though he has already sent Creon to Delphi, has time to listen to and accommodate the pain and fears of his plague-besieged subjects. Similarly, Hamlet has time to brood, to be called to action by the ghost and, since his delay becomes his characteristic tragic trait, has time to assess the validity of the ghost's revelation.

By contrast, Jerry brooks no such indulgences. He must define his character and act upon Peter right away. Like Prospero expresses in *The Tempest*, Jerry's success of his objective involves an opportune time whose urgency "doth depend upon/ A most auspicious star, whose influence/ If now I court not, but omit, my fortunes/ Will ever after droop" (Act 1, Scene 2, lines 181–84).[14] Peter is the "auspicious star" Jerry comes upon and that he takes immediate advantage of in order to make his "fortunes," that is, statement about his isolation. Impelled by similar urgency and opportunity, Eddie pursues his objective of persuading May, with strategies of masculinity, so that their bonds of love could be sealed.

One of the approaches that the playwright often takes to counter the intensity of one-acts so as to allow the audience to prepare itself for the onslaught, so to speak, is to find a way of holding his characters in silence for a few seconds at curtain or lights, that is, before dialogue. That way, the audience could have the time to assess and absorb the condition or situation of the characters before the central character begins to pursue his or her objective. Both Edward Albee and, especially, Sam Shepard create this atmosphere in *Zoo Story* and *A Fool for Love*—Jerry assesses his victim before moving in on him and launching his attack; Eddie and May are held in a pose of seeming hopelessness for a few seconds.

THEME

Another factor for consideration in making distinction between a one-act form and a full-length's is the theme, that physical or visual manifestation of the abstract idea—the original idea/note that strikes the psyche of the playwright. Without trying to confuse, I call it a physical manifestation (an impression), as opposed to the physical expression of it as a play, because technically the characteristic image precedes the expressed dramatic form, even though it may not be consciously perceived until after the initial dramatic expression. But again, because of the incidental nature of the one-act, the scope of the theme for the form is narrower than the all-encompassing scope of a full-length's. Let us, once again, use the already established one-acts as examples.

To reiterate the fact, a theme of a play, because of the dramatic potential it needs to register, should be expressed visually with the subject of the play, and in a clear sentence. For instance, if the subject of *The Zoo Story* is "Isolation," its theme may be expressed, thus: Isolation is a human condition that can make a person be so desperate enough to wish to make a violent statement. In a full-length, while the subject remains the same, the theme may modify to accommodate the multiple-incident scope of the form: Isolation could force somebody to commit violent acts on people, including himself, as a public statement of his desperate needs.

Similarly, we can consider *A Fool for Love*. If its subject is "Bonds of Love," its theme may be expressed thus: "Bonds of Love may be difficult to establish because of familial/societal constraints." In a proposed full-length of the play, that theme may flesh out more, given the extended scope of the form: "Bonds of Love between two people, who seek to stabilize them, may meet with societal taboos that constrain and ultimately destroy the bonds as well as the lovers." In this regard, the possibility of the destruction that is suggested by, and limited to the climax of Shepard's one-act (the outside explosions and the lights that arc, exposing Eddie and May's embrace), may be more crucial in the probable full-length.

The differences, on the one hand, indicate that the limited scope of the one-act, in fact, turns out to be its asset or strong point. On the other hand, what a one-act probably assumes, suggests, or does not have the time to develop, the full-length is able to flesh out extensively. However, all these are probabilities, for a theme may not be clearly perceived by the playwright until the original psychical idea is ritualized in a physical expression. In other words, a theme becomes fully realized only after the play has expressed itself—and this could be after the first draft or subsequent ones. An attempt to do otherwise, by describing the theme before the play is written, may be superficial, unless it is a tentative attempt that is open to change or modification. It is also possible that the same theme can work for a one-act as well as a full-length. In such an instance, given the intensity and the tightness of the one-act form, we can assume the inventive power of the one-act writer at its most crucial.

EXPLORING THE FULL-LENGTH

As a contrast, following our observation of differences between a one-act and a full-length, let us consider the possibility of turning a full-length play into a one-act. For purposes of clarity, let us take Shakespeare's *Othello,* because of the one-act intensity that pervades the play, especially with much of the excrescences of the subplot taken out. First, let us go through its central situation, main given circumstances, subject, theme, objective action, and incidents of that action. It should be stressed again that we have a good idea of these factors only because we know the play; they are not necessarily what should be sought after at the initial stage of creating a new play. They are factors that evolve through a rigorous ritual struggle to explore the components of the idea-note that strikes the psyche.[15]

Situation: A revered black military general, who has secretly married a white daughter of a senator, becomes jealous of his wife through suspicions raised by one of his military staff. (We can identify with such a complex condition of love, because it is human.)

Given circumstances (regarding the central character, Othello): Othello, a black alien but revered general and leader of an Italian army, has fought and won many battles for his adopted country. He has however eloped with Desdemona, a white Italian and daughter of Brabantio, a senator who is adversely sensitive to interracial marriage. (There are other relative circumstances about Othello's background which the playwright invents as he expresses his play, such as details behind his love for Desdemona, his black nomadic and phantasmagoric adventures, and about the crucial handkerchief he has given her).

Subject (what the play is about): Jealousy (which will be used to image and express the theme)

Theme (the articulation of the idea-note that strikes in the playwright's psyche, which in dramatic terms expresses the subject): Jealousy is a compulsive passion that, if allowed to fester, can destroy innocent lives.

Othello's Objective (action he chooses to take when the crisis that might mar his integrity confronts him): To regain his tainted honor by proving his assessment of love is right (Such an objective initiates certain incidents of action, and ritualizes or dramatizes the given circumstances, especially those relating to his character and the handkerchief).

Primary incidents of his action (constituting the plot):

1. Having been accused of illicit marriage to Desdemona, Othello defends his honor to the state of Venice (to the world, so to speak) by proclaiming his love for Desdemona is true and justified.
2. Beset by suspicions and jealousy of his wife's probable infidelity raised by Iago, which taints his honor, Othello demands ocular proof. .
   (These root and developing incidents raise a question—the Major Dramatic Question: Will Othello be able to regain his tainted honor?)
3. (That question will be answered in the climax-incident): Shown a false proof by Iago, Othello in an epileptic fit throws his honor to the wind and swears to kill Desdemona.
4. (The resolution) Seeing that he has been wrong, he kills himself.

The play with its scope of incidents works as a full-length. To try and reduce such an inclusive scope to the exclusive scope of a one-act, obviously, would be difficult. At any rate, many things would have to change. What is possible, however, is to look for a possible situation for a one-act with each incident. In fact, each of the incidents of the above action can work as a one-act. As such, each would have a separate subject, theme, and given circumstances; but none of these, of course, would necessarily be expected to conform with Shakespeare's *Othello*, which is a finished play and is conceived as a full-length by its author.

For instance, we can take the first incident: Othello defends his honor and love for Desdemona to the state of Venice. This incident in a one-act becomes the situation, for which there are given circumstances: Othello has secretly married Desdemona; somebody, perhaps Iago, has secretly raised suspicions of the marriage to Brabantio who therefore has accused Othello of forcing his daughter's hands.

Othello's objective-action may be to regain the trust of Brabantio. This objective demands some strategies (as opposed to the incidents of a full-length), which may or may not achieve his objective. Othello may first plead with Brabantio, man to man, to convince Brabantio that his marriage with Desdemona is legal and based on mutual love. Failing that, Othello may remind Brabantio of his military service to the state of Venice. He may try to gain the support of Cassio, or Iago—either of whom could make the one-act go in different directions. He may also have called for the pastor that married them to demonstrate the sacredness of the marriage, or to disprove accusations of black magic, sexual power, or rape. In fact, various strategies for Othello are open to the creative psyche of the playwright, from which he could make the choice amenable to the idea-note that struck. In fact., since the playwright is limited to an incident, he or she would strive to elicit from the idea-note choices that would be most effective within one location and a short space of time. His or her sense of economy would be at its most critical and challenging. The playwright would also try and avoid the possibility of too many characters or a crowd, since the ultimate challenge of a one-act lies in economy and inventiveness. Too many characters would likely dissipate the energy and tightness of the one-act.

The other incidents that constitute Shakespeare's full-length may follow similar development to create a separate one-act, but we must exercise caution. The difficulty of compressing a full-length to a one-act should by now be obvious, and the way I have gone about it probably should not be encouraged. At any rate, prior knowledge of the full-length may inhibit or limit the inventive resources of the playwright. However, the process should serve to clarify the distinction I have made between the single incident scope of a one-act and the multi-incident scope of a full-length.

OTHER CHARACTERISTICS

The rest of the chapter will be devoted to explaining certain terminologies that are frequently used when analyzing a play's structure, or assessing the components of the creative process. The objective is to see how each term fits into our ritual construct of playwrighting, that is, the creative process that begins in the playwright's psyche. As such, from the point of view of the playwright, I prefer to call these terms ritual implements.

COMPLICATIONS

These are conditions of conflict, both for the playwright and his or her central character. They are provoked by obstacles in the course of the playwright's ritual struggle to define and resolve the ritual needs of the central character. The idea-note that strikes the psyche of the playwright is vibrant with complex resonance of dramatic possibilities. These possibilities remain amorphous until the playwright commits to a physical expression of that idea, a commitment that results in a first draft. In some cases, wrestling with the idea to perceive the possibilities (that is the brooding stage) remains mental for quite some time.

In fact, the ritual struggle is an attempt to come to terms with the dramatic potential of the image evoked by the idea. In an effort to define the image, or break it, as it were, into plausible components, a central focus or character is born, that is, the hypothetical factor proposed not only to relieve the playwright's intense and complicated struggle, but also to define the objective-action capable of channeling the focus or character's needs. In reality, the playwright puts his or her onerous burden on the character, so that the playwright's needs become the character's, and his or her complications (meshed within the idea-note) become the character's. Yet, what makes the needs dramatic are the very complications.

Consequently, when we talk about the complications of the central character, we have taken into consideration the complications of the dramatist whose original idea-note has given birth to the central factor, represented by the central character. We have also taken into consideration the conflicts that the complications assume. To exemplify this further, we can qualify the fact by saying that the drama of the dramatist becomes the drama of its central focus: the drama of Sophocles becomes the drama of Oedipus; the drama of Shakespeare becomes the drama of Hamlet, of Othello, of Prospero. Or, bringing the analogy home to contemporary modern, the drama of Beckett becomes that of Gogo and Didi; that of Albee becomes Jerry's, or George's in *Who's Afraid of Virginia Woolf*; that of Shepard becomes Eddie's or May's, depending on whose side we think the playwright is on; that of Susan-Lori Parks becomes The Foundling Father's, and so on. Thus, any of these characters assume his or her relative playwright's complications and conflicts—which begin from the playwright's psyche.

EMOTION

The dramatic nature of the conceived original idea-note, although difficult to define before the playwright's struggle to image and express it, is, at first and in essence, a fiery ball of raw but complex vibrations or sensations waiting to burst forth in different directions. Indeed, we may argue that all creation replicates this scientific explanation of the creation of the world, except that the creative process also takes on a metaphysical aspect.

With the emergence of a central character, provisional or permanent, the sensations gradually become controlled, and each begins to take an emotional life of its own in other possible and emerging figures or characters. In this regard, the proposed direction of central character, compelled by a proposed objective, is at stake. For this direction takes on certain opinionated, albeit foresightful, values that inevitably attract some opposition or challenge from the values of other life forms, other characters, that manifested from the evolution. The result is the emotion generated by the interrelationships among the life forms or characters, especially in relation to the central character, whose objective action is primal, along with the emotional value he or she brings upon the action.

Hence, there arises the central emotion of the central character and subsidiary emotions that feed it, that is, through the presence and interactions of other characters. For instance, Oedipus is driven by egotistic emotional values, exposing his brand of arrogance, rashness, intolerance, stubbornness, etc., all emoted, variously, through interactions with the characters (the emotional values and objectives) of Teiresias, Jocasta, Creon, and principally with Oedipus himself, that is, his intoxicated objective-action. Similarly, Othello is driven by his ruling passion, jealousy, exposing his militaristic impatience, sensitive temper, and superstitious inclinations, all fueled by the remorselessly evil character of Iago, the innocent, sometime flirtatious persistence of Desdemona, the fawning exuberance and devotion of Cassio, the officious loquaciousness of Emilia, and so forth.

CHARACTER

Embedded in the emotional values that the central character (indeed all characters have the potential) brings to bear on all that he or she encounters are characteristics or traits that drive the character. These characteristics are by no means sacrosanct. On the contrary, they form a complex network of dichotomies that give the character depth of existence. One way of thinking of these binary characteristics is in terms of good and evil, although this generalization may be somewhat broad. Since good and evil are complimentary forces in every human being, it is possible to think these characteristics as various shades of good and evil.

Within the limited space and time of a dramatic expression, some of these characteristics are more defined than others, depending on the oppositional forces that challenge their capacity to control. As such, they could contort into many forms and the emotional values they bring to bear could be driven into various levels or shades of tempo. For the oppositions that challenge their direction could counter directly or indirectly, could even spur on subtly, or blatantly, the central character's characteristics to run against themselves. For example, Oedipus' characteristics become intoxicated and contorted, not only by the seemingly direct characteristic opposition of Creon and Teiresias, but indirectly by the feelings of guilt those characteristics stirred up in Oedipus, propelling him to his own doom. Othello is similarly intoxicated by his own characteristics that he would listen to no voice of reason or plea from Desdemona, but rather to the malice-intended tones of Iago. In fact, the ruling emotions of most central characters, especially tragic heros and heroines, seem one way or another to be driven by an intoxication of their own characteristics, in various shades and tempos of course.

Thus, depending on the character's objective and his or her consistency with that objective, a focused direction that blinds the character's vision to other alternatives, certain intoxications are more specifically dramatized than others. Jerry, in *Zoo Story*, may be said to be driven by an intoxicated desire to make an impactive statement about his isolation, all at the expense of Peter, whose characteristics merely seek to have a moment of peace to himself without offending anyone. On the one hand, this makes Jerry a selfish character; on the other hand, it makes him an experienced individual, one who has come to his resolve through experiences of isolation. Also, one whose perception is accurate in spotting a man that needs help as much as he does.

By contrast, the situation of Eddie or May makes the intoxication more difficult to define. The possibility of the characters living their separate lives is obstructed by the emotional pull that wishes to bind them. This ambivalence would seem to make their relative intoxication less impactive and more confusing. However, given the dynamics of their innocent, illicit relationship, it is possible to identify the differences in intoxication with regard to the characteristics that mold each character. Eddie's rather macho intoxication has driven him so many miles to impose his cowboy ego on May, even though he knows he might be pulled away again, as it has been on previous occasions. At first this attitude looks rather selfish. However, we realize that his return has been encouraged by May's own insecure intoxication of leaving tracks as to where to find her, because of her inability to keep him off her mind. But her intoxicated ambivalence (to oppose or to give way to the pressures of love-bonding) probably smacks of a deeper emotional crisis—her mother had tried to discourage their relationship to no avail, and Eddie's mother reacted to their compulsive bonding by blowing her brains out. These factors at once repel her from Eddie and call attention to her inability to resolve her needs for genuine bonds of love. Ultimately, one could say that both intoxications (Eddie's and May's) complement as well as negate each other to the point of weakening the dramatic potential of each.

Even in *Waiting for Godot*, a play that seems to devalue traditional ways of dramaturgy and in which the central objective seems to be shared by two characters, each central character has characteristics that enhance the emotional value that the character brings to bear not only on the other character but also on the characters passing by and whom they encounter. For instance, Gogo is impossible as he battles with his boots and hates the fact of waiting; Didi frustrates with his accommodating or philosophical viewpoints as he contends with possible head lice and genital problems. But ritual characteristics of both also complement each other to the degree of being interchangeable.

DIALOGUE

In order to express the emotional reaction or viewpoint that derives from character traits of one individual in collision, so to speak, with those of one or more characters, a language (gestural or verbal) understood by most of the individuals is induced for the play. Actually, the language is not necessarily for the benefit of the characters of the play as such, for they do not really have to understand each other, literally or otherwise. In other words, each character can react physically, or psychically, as he or she chooses, uttering sounds that derive purely from the subconscious, that is, from the psyche or the metaphysical reaches that manifest the individual character. In reality, the language, first and foremost, is for the benefit of the playwright, the ritualist who is trying, by any means necessary, to find relief and direction from the amorphous confusion that first defines the idea-note that strikes the psyche. For the characters that manifest from the idea-note, along with the characteristic emotions that describe their individuality, must be coerced into existence by a language (gestural or verbal) the playwright understands. Often, however, it is the language of the public the playwright envisions as the audience of his or her play, and this would explain the need for translations when the play travels to a different cultural locality and audience. When this happens, the playwright has little or no control over a language he or she may not understand.

The playwright-language factor can probably be better explained by the challenge of the one-act monologue. Here, the emotional reaction/viewpoint of the single character, although is simplified by the narrative of the given circumstance, desperately seeks in the present time of the play the reaction/viewpoint of another character, as a sounding board, for its narrative and emotional drive. Finding none, it seeks that can be motivated by a "stage audience." Language of the single character in the presence of a "stage audience" clearly incorporates words, gestures, movement, etc.—which are all the more important to the playwright and his or her monologist because there are no other resources, namely individual characters, for both to feed on, except the emotional drive generated by the "stage audience."

As stated earlier, the playwright's objective aligns with that of his or her central character in the creative process of expression of the idea that strikes the playwright's psyche. In a one-act monologue, the playwright's objective aligns with that of the single character to express the given circumstances and the present action or experience of the monologue. Since there is no intrusion of other characters and their emotional viewpoints, it would seem the playwright of the one-act monologue could choose any language he or she wishes. However, to be able to have full control of the single character, the playwright must use a language he or she and the character understand, a language which, by extension, should also serve the theater audience for which the monologue is intended.

GESTURES

Technically, gestures ascribed or implied in play texts are the province of the actor. However, it must not be forgotten that they derive from the playwright, part of the language that has evolved with the dramatic expression from the idea-note that strikes in the playwright's psyche. In this regard, they are codes that are embedded in the expression, codes which the reader must feel, or the director and the actor must find and give physical expression to so that the theater audience can have a better understanding of what the playwright intends. Shakespeare's plays, for instance, easily demonstrate this built-in codes within the playwright's language.

On a final note, these ritual components of dramatic writing put us back to the beginning and the source—the generated idea-note in the creative psyche of the playwright. Our contention is that all the components are present initially when the idea-note strikes the psyche, that metaphysical arena of creative/dramatic engagement of the potential playwright. At that initial stage, the components of the idea, or the tone colors of the note, along with their dramatic implications, must first be felt and understood by the playwright, the primal ritual quester and interpreter of the *illud tempus*, before they could be expressed to serve the playwright's aesthetic needs—be it political, historical, satirical, ritual, etc. To be able to give expression effectively, the playwright should try and concretize the idea-note into an image. This would enable the playwright to locate the potential focus, the character that first engages the playwright with a monotonic/monologic, singular objective capable of expressing the character's situational circumstances. Then, through a ritual struggle, the playwright gains access to the speaker's ritual/dramatic drive, and the challenges that confront the drive, challenges that raise problems of emotion, character, and language. With continued ritual deliberation, the playwright gradually expresses his or her drama, which could remain a one-act monologue or, through intrusion of other characters, could develop into a regular one-act or a full-length structure.

NOTES

1. Tennessee Williams, *The Glass Menegerie* (New York: Dramatist Publishing, 1975)

2. Louis Catron summarizes well the challenges of a one-act play in *Playwriting: Writing, Producing and Selling Your Play* (Prospect Heights, Il: Waveland Press, 1984), 51–60

3. Sam Shepard, *Fool for Love and Other Plays*, 27 See comments on this in chapter 2, xxx

4. *Fool for Love*, 54.

5. *Fool for Love*. See 54–55.

6. *Fool for Love*, 55.

7. Other critics seem to associate Jerry with the Prophet Jeremiah—see Ruby Cohn, *Edward Albee*, in *University of Minnesota Pamphlets on American Writers* (MN: University of Minnesota Press, 1969), 9. This conflicts with my own reading in terms of what I think is an important link with Peter the apostle.

8. Edward Albee, *The Zoo Story* and *The Sandbox*, 27

9. For the ritual implications of the play, see Mary Castiglie Anderson's "Ritual and Initiation in *The Zoo Story*," in *Edward Albee: Interviews and Essays* ed. Julian Wasserman et al (Houston, TX: University of St. Thomas, 1983), 93–108.

10. Shakespeare, *The Tragedy of Macbeth*, ed. Nicholas Brooke (Oxford: Clarendon Press, 1990), 124–25.

11. See *Fool for Love and Other Plays*, 32–33

12. See ch. 3, 59–60.

13. Frederick C. Mish, et al., editors *Webster's Ninth New Collegiate Dictionary* (MA: Merriam-Webster Inc., 1986).

14. Shakespeare, *The Tempest*, 111.

15. See Appendix II for the analysis of some of the other plays discussed in this book.

Conclusion

Ritual Efficacies:
The Illud Tempus Script

Any creative expression, in an effort to realize itself more fully, thrives on revisions—attempts to modify, refocus, rethink parts or all of the initial vision that spawned the expression. More crucial this fact for the creative process of playwriting, that is, given its effort to strikes into permanence, in language and visual codes, a realistic portrayal of human images, emotions, struggles, movements, etc. The first physical rendering of the ritual registers (the *illud tempus* script) through a workable central focus, from the idea that struck, often might be realized cluttered, clumsy, confusing, or unstructured. It therefore often requires several subsequent ritual immersions to give the expression its complete lucid form.

A play for the stage is meant to be performed to a live theater audience; hence, it is advisable that dramatic expression in its development through the ritual immersions be tested in stages of performance-workshops preferably, by experienced actors, to various audiences. This way the playwright is able to engage constructive and live feedbacks helpful to the playwright's revision process. Only then is the play ready for full performance.

Yet, a play ready for a full production is not necessarily free from revisions. A director sensitive to the playwright's vision, and to the dramatic possibilities of the theatrical space, may help further widen or extend the vision of the playwright through the participation of professional actors that the director assembles. The playwright should not see this as a detriment but an opportunity or a challenge for him to re-immerse himself yet again. I have received such help from many directors, although not without resistance—which is a natural human reaction.

Although what the playwright does to his or her realized script is beyond the scope of this book, a professional production of a playwright's work is the ultimate desirable achievement. As such, this should be the primary objective of the playwright, that is, after his or her script has gone through the stages of workshop tests already stated. It is only after such a realized production should a playwright attempt to publish the work. Such a production presumes some kind of working trust between the director and playwright. It presumes the sensitivity of an experienced director who is able to dialogue with the playwright about the potential (strengths and weaknesses) of the new work, and conceive his or her director's concept within the playwright's vision with the view to enlarging that vision. On the other hand, the production presumes an accommodation by the playwright of the experienced discretion of the director and his suggestions for possible re-visioning, necessary for the full potential of the *illud-tempus* script. For, even though the playwright has previously undergone a series of re-immersions, he or she should be alert to the technical or creative demands of the stage-space or stage-craft—which, alternately, improves the playwright's script.

Ultimately, the watch-word for the playwright is clarity of vision and expression, a clarity that presumes the interpretation of the actor and the audience, that is, the human communicator and communicant of the *illud tempus* script. Whether the expression that manifests is a realist or anti-realist, it has to communicate to the human element that receives its message, so to speak. It is not enough to simply strike or bombard the senses of the audience with words and images–the Futurists have done it, to no avail. Without a distinctive thread of thematic or objective action that helps the actor and the audience (a paying audience for that matter) to make connections with the script, no realistic interpretation, therefore communication, is possible.

Appendix I

Organic Practicum: *Development Exercises*

The following exercises represent a gradual approach to inciting the imaginative and creative resources of an individual intending to write a play. The step-by-step procedure begins with locating the idea that strikes the creative psyche and transforming that idea into a workable dramatic image. Through this image, a dramatic situation with a possible central character becomes visible, a character capable at first of emoting a monotonic/monologic utterance relating to the situation. Thus the page or stage space is set, from where a play develops its various scopes—a one-act monologue, a regular one-act, or a full-length. Of course, the approach is by no means the only way to generate a dramatic response or create a dramatic expression, but it is my hope that the exercises with their organic intention will harness, rather than destroy, the power of invention. As such, the exercises should offer a new dimension that is provocative and yet practical in eliciting the right response to playwriting.

1. *Probing the* Illud tempus, *or the psyche*
   a. Through music:
      —Listen to your favorite choice of music—classical, jazz, rock, etc, preferably with eyes closed so that you can be more alert to the tones and colors of the sound. Avoid music with words as much as possible.
      —Record words, or phrases (preferably emotive) that express your feelings while listening.
   b. Through Visual Art :
      —Observe an artwork (painting, sculpture, print), preferably abstract, that captures your interest at an exhibition, in books, reception halls, etc.

—Let your mind be alert and be focused in contemplation to determine why the work strikes you.
 —Record words, or phrases (preferably emotive) that express your feelings as you contemplate.
 c. Through other expressions:
 —You can go through the same process as in (a) or (b) with other artistic expressions, such as dance.
2. *Imaging or Concretizing*
 a. Words:
 —Take any word you have recorded in Exercise 1, for example, Love or Anger.
 —Concretize it into a visual or physical expression. In other words, write down sentences or phrases that show what the word evokes for you visually or physically. Avoid creating an abstract as much as possible; use words that express what you could see, touch, hear, smell, taste, etc. Also, you can use the descriptive or the narrative mode.
 Example:—Love is like a red, red rose that blossoms in the glooms of autumn (descriptive)
 —Sheltering itself from a windy storm under the ruins of a wooden shed, a white and black cat suckles its kittens (narrative)
 b. Phrases:
 —Pick any of the phrases you have recorded. More likely it is an abstract. Concretize the abstract as in (a), or if the phrase recorded is potentially concrete and visual, improve on it by making it more consciously concrete and physical.
 Example:—Corruption of power: A head of a lion invaded by maggots depicted on a picketing placard (descriptive).
 —The president of the nation makes the people pay "presidential palace taxes," which go directly into his bank account (narrative).
 As you can see, inherent in these images are potential ingredients for drama. In other words, they are dramatic images.
3. *Exploring the Dramatic*
 a. Character:
 Now focus on the visually concretized sentence or phrase you have created. Imagine or invent an individual or character within the visual emanations of the sentence or phrase. You may ask the following questions that could help you to invent:
 —Is there anybody involved in some action in the picture (for instance, with the red roses, or the black and white cat suckling her kittens)? If so, who is he or she? What is he or she doing, or has done (to the roses, or the cat)? If possible, identify, or characterize the person, and

what he or she does. See how the person moves, how he or she looks, speaks and gestures. Is there any visible characteristic trait? With the lion-head on picketing placard, it is easy enough to see an individual or individuals carrying pickets. Who is the leader, and how is he or she conducting the picketing? What age group are the picketers? What is the immediate cause for picketing? And what or who do the symbols on the pickets represent? Does the lion-head represent a powerful head of state, president, governor, or mayor? How corrupt is he or she? The maggots would seem to signify the debilitating or destructive nature of his corruption. Is the corruption affecting the economy, the infrastructure or social structure of the state? What may be the implications for the man or woman carrying the picket and the group of individuals with the person? In fact, something of a situation should begin to form.

b. Situation:

With luck, you now have an individual or individuals in mind, a person or persons with some distinguishing characteristics. However, if you are not certain and such individual or individuals appear to just exist with no clear identity, don't worry, that identity will materialize later as you continue to explore the dramatic.

Having acknowledged the visual potential of the imaging sentence or phrase, see whether you can establish an incident or a situation for the individual of the image. It is important the situation is not simply a situation, but one with dramatic possibilities, that is, one that raises consequential factors.

Example: — A woman has been looking for her black and white cat for several days (a situation — here a dramatic potential is not apparent).

— A woman, who has accused her next door neighbor as responsible for the disappearance of her cat, discovers the cat suckling her newly born under her own house (dramatic situation). Or, perhaps more dramatic, the neighbor thus accused discovers the cat under her accuser's house.

— A man is carrying a placard with a picture of a lion's head invaded by maggots (situation).

— A man, carrying a placard with a picture of a lion's head invaded by maggots, is picketing outside the head of state's mansion along with his comrades (dramatic situation).

The next stages of dramatic structure do not necessarily follow the previous ones in order of development. However, they are possible indications of the creative process worth thinking about. As stated, these elements of structure do not have to be considered until much later, perhaps after the first draft when the playwright has a better understanding of what he or she wants to write about.

c. Subject:

What is your play about? Not the title of the play, but what you are assuming you want to write about. Is it about "Untested Love," about "Jealousy," about "Terrorism"? You have probably scribbled some of these subjects in your journal or notebook, as things you would like to write about in future. Sometimes it helps to have a subject in mind, if only provisionally. For instance:

— You have a situation in mind or you have actually expressed it, does the situation initially tell you what your play might be about?
— Consider the first situation in section (b), can you think of possible subjects for that situation? Is it about "Discrimination" or "Prejudice"?
— Think of other situations with a dramatic potential. Then see whether you can come up with a subject.

Now, even if you cannot state the subject of your play, you can at least learn how to access it, using already existing plays as examples, as we have done throughout this book.

  (i) Read or re-read any play of your choice.
  (ii) Consider the central character and what the play, overall, is saying about him or her, what the play is about, that is, its subject.
  (iii) Try to state this subject in one word or a short phrase — it is the word or phrase that enables us to relate to the play's idea or theme. Or, in terms of our trope, it is the key that strikes the idea-note in the psyche.
  (iv) Read or re-read other plays and follow the same process.

d. Theme:

The subject-key strikes the note-idea. Knowing the key is to identify what it registers and its full potential. Knowing what your play is about will enable you to use that subject to explain the idea of the play you have in mind. Stating a theme is a way of explaining the subject in dramatic terms, that is, how the subject plays out in action — it allows you to come to grips with the dramatic content, or what you want to express. However, on a cautionary note, subject and theme at the initial stages of playwriting, at first, may be very elusive to express; often it is not necessary to consider them seriously until after the creative thrust of your first draft. They allow the playwright to engage subsequent ritual re-immersions into the *illud tempus* for subsequent drafts.

But suppose, tentatively, you know what your play is about, and suppose you have an individual in mind with whom you wish to relate the

subject. Suppose that subject (from what we know of a situation in section b.) is "Discrimination," and you have an individual in mind to relate this subject to, the question is:
— How do you see this individual (perhaps nameless at the moment) try to express the subject of discrimination through the play, in spite of the obstacles (conflicts) that oppose the individual?
— What is the possible consequence for the individual's insistence in pursuing the subject of discrimination?
— Does he or she succeed? If so, what happens? If not, what happens?

Taking these questions into consideration may help you come to grips with the idea-note that strikes with the key-subject of "Discrimination" thus:
— Discrimination is an attitude that can make a person perform insane acts that eventually causes unnecessary loss of lives.

Or, in a lighter mood:
— Discrimination may function as a boomerang, launched by the victimizer on the victim, which comes back to deal an embarrassing blow on the victimizer. (One presumes it comes back after its unsuccessful attempt to strike the victim).

Learn how to express a theme with a subject from an established text, as follows:
   (i) Pick up and re-read a play you have read.
   (ii) Express, in one word or a short phrase, what the play is about, that is, its subject.
   (iii) With that subject, express the idea of the play, taking into consideration the central character, his or her central obstacle or conflict, and what eventually happens to the individual as a result of the pursuit of his or her objective. Express the idea as a general statement for any individual as opposed to a specific character.
   (iv) Read or re-read other plays and follow the same process.

Caution: You can use the subject to express the theme the best way you can. However, for clarity, it is advisable to use the "subject" as the subject of your sentence. Doing so would enable you to see the dramatic pursuit of the central character clearly and unmistakable. This is a director's approach to the text that I have found to be beneficial to the playwright's vision.

4. *Emoting the Monotonic Monologue*

The idea-note that is struck by the subject-key, loaded with dramatic possibilities, is in need of expressing itself. Its first expression through a possible central character vis-à-vis the playwright, even if only for a short time, is often singular or monotonic and therefore monologic. Such monotonic monologue can develop dramatically with its singular voice into a one-act monologue or flesh out in dialogic exchange with other character or characters. Understanding the process of this development may help the playwright come to terms with dramaturgical problems he or she is likely to encounter.

a. First, you should come to terms with the values of an ordinary speech or a monologue, so you can understand its capabilities.
   — Pick a moderately long speech or a monologue from a play. Any of Shakespeare's monologues should do, such as Hamlet's "To be or not to be." You may also make up a speech in your head, but it must be focused, meaning it must have an objective or purpose. At any rate, so should any speech you chose, whether composed and written down, or selected from an already existing play.
   — Read it a couple of times to yourself, trying to understand what it is saying.
   — Memorize about four or five lines of the monologue.
   — Then close your eyes, and say the few lines, slowly, intoned in a monotone, two or three times.
   — Listen. Perhaps something motivates it, and it is being directed to somebody or something. This is the moment to find out.
   — Each time, try and listen to yourself in relation to what you are saying, giving value to every word. Because your eyes are closed and your attention is not diverted by any inflection or speech pattern, you are likely to appreciate the meaning of every word in relation to one another. More important, you are more aware of yourself, and you feel more confident with what you are saying, because virtually, nobody is listening to you but yourself. In this regard, you are not afraid of making mistakes, you are not afraid of the implications of the speech to anyone else. It is as if you are bearing your mind out to yourself, as honestly as you can, about a particular something, perhaps regarding somebody else. It is your own opinion and damn the consequences.

   This is the way a monologue should work—as your own (or the character's) honest opinion, and meaning exactly what you say. Therefore you (or your character) should say exactly what you mean.

b. Now, let us emote a monologue from an idea that has struck. As stated, the idea-note that strikes the psyche, even though it is potent with dramatic possibilities, at first or in its first raw thrust, often expresses itself in a monotone of a single voice/character before other characters, if they exist, come into play. One way of stimulating or beginning to access the dramatic possibilities of the idea is to encourage that monotone to express itself. For by so doing, the playwright not only confronts most of the challenges of playwriting, but also he or she begins to come to terms with the demands of the one-act monologue to be written.

— Choose any of the situations you have previously come up with.
— Consider the situation. For instance: A woman who has accused her neighbor as responsible for her cat's disappearance, suddenly discovers the cat suckling her newly born under her own house. You should have some glimpse of a character (the Woman) who, for the moment, could be considered as central to your situation, although ultimately may not be.
— Try and identify the character tentatively, by inventing a background (biographical, official, familial, material, etc.) for her.
— Consider the situation again in relation to the character (the woman). It not only establishes an accusation, but also identifies the recipient of the accusation, her neighbor. Yet that accusation falls flat with the discovery of the cat under her own house.
— There are many possibilities of emoting. If she is still looking for the cat, she could emote the accusation—her real feelings regarding her neighbor. A witch who has been responsible for the disappearance of other cats in the neighborhood ? If she discovers the cat under her house, what could she emote? Does she now feel any guilt and seeks some closure with her conscience, or is she trying to justify her former beliefs? Could the neighbor have been responsible for putting the cat back under the house? Many things are possible to initiate the monologue. Let your power of imagination invent wildly.
— Follow the same process with the neighbor. She has been accused of killing the cat, but now she has found the cat under her accuser's house. This is her moment to unleash her feelings about the accuser. Identify her background, and let her tell her own side of the situation. What's her objective? Is it to prove the woman wrong, or to plan some sort of revenge?
— Check the monologue each character has expressed. Remember, either character should have an objective for emoting. In other words, the monologue should not only be motivated, it should also have a purpose. This will be helpful in the next stage of development.
— Choose different situations and follow the same process of identifying characters and letting each character emote his or her story regarding a situation that involves one other character that is not present.

5. *Developing a One Act Monologue*
    — You should now have at least two characters, each having emoted his or her version of a situation but in the absence of the other character. Each is prompted by something and is with an objective.
    — However, to turn that monotonic monologue into a dramatic expression, you need to be conscious of, although not necessarily all at once, at least the following:
    (i) The present time of the situation.
    (ii) A "stage audience," that is, a virtual listener to whom, or to which the monologue is being addressed.
    (iii) A more formal identity of the character.
    (iv) Assuming you have already thought of it, what initiated the character to speak, and what his or her objective is.
    (v) A location at the present time of the play.
    These considerations can be induced by questions.
    — Choose any of the monologues you wish. Ask questions such as:
    — What is the woman doing at the present time of emoting? And what is she trying to achieve (that is, her objective)?
    — What motivates her into emoting at the present time?
    — Where is she at this present time? Why is she there?
    — What are the things in the present location that might help her to focus her objective? Look around the location to find out.
    — Does the woman have a name? Or is she, as Woman, supposed to represent all or most women in general? Name of a character (the name that suits her character traits) often suggests itself intuitively. But since it is also part of the idea-note that struck, you may need to wrestle with the psyche for it.
    — To whom is she emoting a complaint or her objective? To herself? To the picture of the cat, or the cat's food that has not been eaten for two days? To the theatre audience?
    — If it is to the theatre audience, whom do they represent—her imagined other neighbors, or some jury?
    To be able to answer such questions, which pose problems of verisimilitude to the playwright, will enable the playwright to engage his or her objective of writing the play.
    Follow the same process with other situations and other characters, and other monotonic monologues.
6. *Expanding the scope of the one-act monologue*
    Now, you want to expand the one-act monologue to a regular one-act with at least two characters. You have in fact already set this in motion—that is, by making two characters, conditioned by the same situation, emote

their feelings separately, without the presence of the other. If you have not done this so far, now is the time to do so.

So, you have two versions of the same situation or story. Perhaps now you can put the two characters together. How will they react when they meet? Similar challenges apply:
— What motivates their meeting?
— At what location are they meeting?
— Who is the central character? Who has the stronger objective, one that is central to the drama being expressed? Does he or she have a name suited to his or her character?
— What is this central character's objective and what obstacles (from the other character, from himself or herself, from things around the character) seem to confront that objective?
— How does the other character react or play against this central character's attempts to achieve his or her objective?

7. *Expanding the Ritual Scope to a Full-length*

Expanding the dramatic scope of your play to a full-length means extending the situational boundaries to accommodate more than one incident, as opposed to the restrictive single incident of a one-act. Again, similar problems of structure apply. However, the following questions may help to wrestle with the problems:
— Can I make the situation I have be inclusive of more than one incident for the central character? Or, can my central character's objective accommodate two or more situational incidents?
— The point of attack of the one-act, that is, the point where the central character begins to follow his or her objective-action at the present time of the play, is probably focused to engage a limited time-span. For instance, the time-span of Oedipus Rex, without the choral odes, works like the concentrated but limited time-span of a one-act — without the chorus, it is possible to conflate its many incidents to one. In fact, you may use such a play as an exercise in compressing or expanding a situation. If you are thinking of exploring the one-act frame you initially conceived to a possible full-length, the question is, how can the one-incident situation of the one-act, with its limited time-span, widen so as to accommodate more possible incidents?
— The background circumstances that you have wrested from the idea-note that struck have many potential incidents. With a clear idea of these circumstances, at what point does your possible central character begin to confront his or her objective action? Do you see the possibility of more than one incident from that point? Sophocles pitches Oedipus' point of attack at a late stage in the given circum-

stances of Oedipus' story, yet he is able to accommodate incidents with Teresias, Jocasta, the messenger from Corinth, and Shepherd who knows the truth.
— Given the latitude of the new situation, what other characters now begin to make themselves known? How do these characters relate to the objective-action of the possible central character? Bear in mind that the central character of the limited one-act does not have to be that of the extensive full-length.

Such questions may help you begin to focus your full-length. On the other hand, as with the intentions of giving form to any play, you may delay asking these questions, until your intuition has been allowed to express the first draft of the full-length.

8. *Other Applicable Factors*

Your play, whether a monotonic monologue, a one-act monologue, a regular one-act or a full-length must gravitate towards some high point in terms of its conflicts, which then get resolved one way or another. You may consider the following questions as you try to engage the challenges of the creative process that impede your progress, or objective to realize your expression:

— Does the central character have a focused and consistent objective?
— Are his or her dominant character traits clearly defined?
— How do the other characters relate to the central character's situation and objective? How do their relationships with the central character reveal their own character traits?
— What is the central conflict? And how do the other conflicts, if any, relate to this?
— Does the play have a clear subject? What is it?
— Does the theme (the central idea) relate with the subject? How does it? Define it.
— At what point is it clear your central character will or will not achieve his or her objective? This moment usually defines the climax.
— If your central character achieves the objective, what does he or she do? If your central character does not achieve the objective, what does he or she do? The answer usually expresses the resolution

Asking questions constantly, questions that challenge the creative process itself will help you through the difficulties of expression.

Appendix II

A One-Act Monologue

I have chosen to include an example of a one-act monologue, written by one of my promising undergraduate students, as a supplement to our earlier discussion of the form, in chapter five.

The monologue grew out of an exercise usually given in my advanced undergraduate workshop—letting a possible central character emote his or her thoughts on a developing situation and a background of arising circumstances from biographical sketches invented for the character. In terms of the ritual emanations of the creative process we have been considering, it is an attempt to give expression to the monotonic monologue that vibrates from the idea-note that strikes the psyche. The exercise helps the playwright to come to terms with his or her possible central character's objective-action, possible fate process (at the present time of the play), possible conflicts, etc., all of which may extend the playwright's vision for a possible one-act (monologue or regular), or a full-length. Kelley Girod's vision follows just that—her emoted monologic monologue results first in the following one-act monologue, then in a regular one-act with two or three characters, and finally, by inventing further (in subsequent ritual immersions), in a full-length.

However, the monologue itself underwent so many revisions in the attempt to overcome the challenges posed by the form, such as resolving the action of the present time of the play, what motivates the monologue and whom it is addressing, and focusing the various ritual elements of structure. These, in fact, are challenges that confront the playwright in general in any creative process of playwriting. The limitations of the form make these factors more critical but rewarding for the playwright in understanding their dramatic functionality.

I have chosen the monologue by the very fact of the unpretentious and yet subtle simplicity of its objective-action, its uncomplicated given circumstances, and its straightforward ritual (dramatic) process. Read it, see whether you can identify its ritual registers of subject, theme, objective action, etc. Kelley has also utilized a "stage audience" that helps her and the character emote naturally and unforcedly within the location and present action. Can you identify this?

First Date
by
Kelley Girod

We are in the room of a twelve-year old girl, Millie. Of a boring beige color, the room is sparsely furnished and decorated. In the middle is a single bed. The left wall has a big tug-and pull window opening into the courtyard of the duplex apartment. Also in the room are a desk with chair, and a dresser. Some clothes are hanging over the chair and on the desk is a cell-phone. The only thing with some color in the room is inside her closet door, which is open—a poster of a medieval knight in shining armor, kneeling to his princess. Clothes are falling out of the closet, as if someone has been tearing through it, looking for something to wear.

>   Millie
>
>   (Pacing back and forth in her room. She has on
>   a black dress that hangs off her shoulder, and no
>   shoes. Her hair is up in curlers and she is wear-
>   ing heavy make-up. She halts, looks towards the
>   window and then casts a glance at her wrist-
>   watch)

Oh God! It's late. He's probably there by now! I'm going!

>   (She frantically rips the curlers out of her hair
>   and puts on a pair of low-heeled shoes that are
>   beside her bed. She goes to the window, unlocks
>   it, lifts it up, puts her head out, and quickly with-
>   draws. Frustrated, she stares out for a few sec-
>   onds, then slams the window shut)

Dammit! She always has to get her way! I decide my life, not her!

>   (Leaves the window, paces a bit, then plops
>   down on the bed, sitting on her teddy bear.
>   Quickly rises)

Oh, sorry Roo.

>   (Pulls a big teddy bear from underneath her and
>   hugs it, then holds it out to make an eye contact
>   with it)

I'm just really pissed right now. Mama has to make things so hard. God! You should have seen the show with Aunt Mattie just now . . . Big red face and boo hoo, all to keep me here, in this prison! Of all the things she's done, this is just too much... She must know about tonight, she has to—all that crying, and Aunt Mattie rubbing her back, trying to calm her down. Said something about some rape. What rape? She was trying to scare me, that's all! How could she, how dare she! . . . A cheap trick!

> (She leans back, pulls out the locket around her neck and opens it)

That's right Chris, they're just trying to scare me, keep me from coming to see you tonight.

> (looks at Roo)

You remember my date tonight don't you Roo? My date with Chris Majors. Oh, Roo, I think I love him. Not stupid puppy love, real love.

> (Urgent look comes over her face)

God, he's waiting, and I'm sitting here like a scaredy cat!

> (She jumps up, sets the bear on the bed, fixes her dress and looks at her watch again)

Dammit! I'm supposed to be at the park by now! Hope he hasn't left . . . What if he left? . . . He'll hate me! Maybe break up with me!

> (The thought makes her nervous and frantic. She goes to the window, but doesn't open it)

God, it's so dark out Roo . . . Mama says bad things happen at night. Things like . . . rape. Mama . . . raped?

> (The thought hits her for the first time)

Mama was raped? When? Where? . . . Couldn't be! Where? . . . Even if she was, what's that got to do with me? I'm not gonna get . . . Mama was raped? I heard it, Roo. I heard them talking about it—her bedroom door was slightly open. Aunt Mattie was telling her she had to get over it. Auntie says, that's just what the man wants her to do, to never forget it. She says Mama lets him do it over and over again every time she cries about it, and she mustn't allow that . . . Yes, Mama has been crying a lot, I thought it was just because she misses Daddy—he's been away for so long now, you know, Roo, like he does, goes off to work at some place . . . Yes, that's what it is, she just misses Daddy. I didn't hear anything about a rape, until now!

> (Moving away from the window)

But it seemed real Roo, her tears and stuff I mean. Gosh, what an act! She was hanging all over Aunt Mattie, like she couldn't hold herself up . . .

> (Thoughtfully, as the idea hits her)

But, why night Roo? Why does Chris want to meet me at night? To go to some party he says . . .

> (As she walks around the room, she casts her eyes momentarily on the poster of the knight and the princess)

Well, it doesn't matter if it's at night., Chris will protect me. He wouldn't do anything to hurt me, would he? No, he's my knight in shining armor . . . His green eyes sparkle Roo, like the knight's! Looks like someone put little chunks of gold in them. And his voice, gosh . . . so smooth! . . . When he talks I just feel so relaxed, like he's singing a lullaby or something. Oh, he's wonderful, absolutely perfect. Chris would never . . . he's not like that. Mama just staged the whole thing up—you know how she is, Roo, when she tries to tell me everything is bad.

> (mocks her mother's voice)

"Millie, no candy, you'll get a cavity!" "Millie, no parties, bad things happen when kids get in groups." "Millie no phone, no tv!" And her favorite, "No boys! Boys lie! Boys have a one track mind! Boys only want that one thing." Well, I know what boys do and do not want! I'm old enough to know better! . . . Why can't she see that Roo?

> (The cell phone on her desk begins to flash.)

That's Chris, waiting for so long! I'm coming, I'm coming.

> (Picks up the cell-phone, but does not answer it)

He gave this to me, so he'll always know where I am.

> (She dashes back to the window and pulls it up. She looks out, frantically swats at something, and quickly pushes the window back down)

Damn bee! Why can't he fly somewhere else! Sign of bad luck!

> (Checks to see whether the bee has disappeared)

Bees have always been bad luck for me, Roo, ever since that incident in first grade—must have brushed over a nest on the playground, but there, everywhere . . . Bees! That day I failed a math test! . . .

> (She walks away from the window, and sets the cell phone down on the dresser. She sits down on the bed next to the bear, which she subconsciously picks up and begins to squeeze rather nervously)

Chris tells me strange stories. He told me one day at school that he had a dream about me. A dream about me... Said I was wearing a red two piece, and me and him were on a beach alone and . . .

> (She pauses embarrassed to repeat the rest)

He was laughing about it. Gosh, I felt like such a prude! . . . But why did he tell me that story? . . . H'm! Mama says guys have a one track mind. If one has a one track mind, does one dream about stuff like that all the time, like . . . like sex and stuff? . . .

A One-Act Monologue 145

(She hugs Roo)

No, Chris would never hurt a fly, he loves me. He told me so, two days after we met. Only two days, can you believe that! We met in the library, you see. Came up to me and told me I had a pretty smile. He just kept staring at me with those shinning green eyes. He said, "I was going to ask you if you have a boyfriend, but why bother? I know the answer is probably yes." What a line! He made me laugh. Well, of course, I told him I didn't have any. Then he said that I was the prettiest girl he'd ever seen. He asked if I would come back to the library the next day, and I did. He said he thought about me all night long and couldn't sleep, hear that Roo? Said it was love, and I agreed. It was love that kept him up all night, and he knew it.

> (She smiles and gets up; her smile soon fades; she sits back down)

Mama says guys will say anything to get what they want . . . That's not true, she doesn't know anything about Chris!

> (Cell-phone lights beep again on the dresser. She gets up, anxious, but does not move towards the window)

God, what Roo? What do I do? I do love him . . . I think. See how Mama's confusing me! . . . Gosh Roo, you should see how the girls envy me! All of them want to be friends with me because he is my boyfriend. I can't disappoint him? . . . I'm going!

> (Goes to the mirror on her dresser. She checks her hair and makeup, grabs her make-up bag and the cell phone, then goes to the window. She lifts up the window, but stalls again)

What am I doing?

> (She glances at the clothes hanging over her desk chair. Becomes more frustrated)

What she's doing to me!

> (Cell-phone stops beeping. Millie clumps back to the dresser, hopelessly puts down the make-up bag and phone. On an impulse, she turns round to the chair and begins throwing the clothes piece by piece)

Always setting my clothes out! Treats me just like a baby! I'm not a baby! I don't need her to tell me when to eat, when to sleep, who I can and can't talk to! I'm a woman, I decide my life! . . . The embarrassment, Roo . . . Millie's mama doesn't let her do this, Millie's mama doesn't let her do that! Millie is a prude. She doesn't kiss, she hasn't even gotten a period yet. Don't invite her to any parties 'cause she can't come anyway! . . . Laughing behind my back all the time! . . . Chris is right, I shouldn't listen to her. She just doesn't want me to have fun.

Chris says—

                      (Her voice suddenly cracks)

Chris says . . .

                      (She becomes nervous at the images that interrupt her thoughts. She crumbles on her knees and starts to cry)

Horrible! . . . Mama told Aunt Mattie the man was horrible. She said he whispered to her ear that her ass was pretty . . . horrible . . . Chris says . . . Horrible! He would lick his lips, would ask me what I was wearing when we talked on the phone at night. His friends would laugh and wink when they see us behind the school.

                      (Regards her dress)

Told me to dress sexy tonight, for him.

                      (As she gets up languidly, goes to the window and looks out without opening it)

Mama said the man was handsome, had violet eyes. I heard it. Violet eyes, can you imagine that? Prettier than Chris' green eyes.

                      (Turns round sharply as if to refocus details she has allowed up till then to blur)

Mama lifted up her shirt, showed Aunt Mattie the big red cuts on her belly . . . I saw it! Said the man pushed her down so hard in the gravel! . . . Roo, can a beautiful man really do such bad things?

                      (Cell-phone on the dresser lights up again)

Tomorrow he'll tell his friends what he did to me, will write my name on the bathroom wall. Add it to his list, I guess . . .

                      (Horrified as the recognition dawns on her. With a struggle:)

My Mama was raped.

                      (Deeply hurt, she goes to pick up the phone, goes to the window, lifts it up and throws it out. She unlocks the locket around her neck and throws it out also. She calmly closes the window and locks it, then goes to sit on the bed next to Roo, picks him up and fondly squeezes him)

You're the only friend I have.

                      (More in a recognition of her own salvation from the same fate)

My mama was raped Roo . . . Raped.

A One-Act Monologue 147

                    (Crying softly, she sets Roo down, gets up and
                    begins to pick up the clothes she threw away, in
                    preparation for bed)

Blackout

Now that you've read the play, perhaps, as in a regular play, you've been able to identity the ritual registers of the structure:

—What is the subject and theme of the monologue?
—What is the objective of Millie?
—Does this objective describe a thread of an action? What is it?
—What obstacles confront Millie's objective, creating conflict?
—What is the major dramatic question imposed by ths action?
—To what climax does that action gravitate?
—How is the action realized? Does Millie achieve her objective?
—What resolution does Millie describe?
—What are the limitations of the form, and how has the playwright tried to overcome them?

Because of the simplicity with which the author expresses the ritual registers of he monologue, these questions should not be difficult to answer. Even so, as with any creative effort in process, there's still room for development, through continued ritual immersions, and feedbacks from workshops. For instance, one feels the urgency of purpose that compels the character's objective still needs attention. Giving Millie more stakes may resolve this.

Apart from this, do you see any other possibilities for improvement?

Perhaps now you can create your own one-act monologue from an established character's emoted thoughts on a situation, arising from the character's sketched background and his or her possible objective.

Appendix III

Ritual Registers: *Analysis of Text*

The following represents a structural breakdown of some of the texts we have been considering, the registration or itemization of the ritual impulses that constitute the idea-note that strikes the psyche. With these, the playwright through ritual immersion is able eventually to realize and shape the dramatic content of his or her creative expression. As implied or stated severally in the previous chapters, these ritual components need not preoccupy the playwright at first, since the initial thrust of creativity, however shapeless it bursts forth to start with, must be allowed a voluntary passage from the metaphysical *illud tempus* of the psyche to the physical arena or space of ritual expression. Structure emerges through rigorous re-immersion, and the understanding of the ritual components embedded in the creative process of that initial thrust. The analysis of these plays only attempts to familiarize the playwright with these components so that they become easy to locate in the playwright's effort to give shape to his or her drama.[1] Each analysis is by no means definitive; it is proposed only to exemplify the development that occurs in the creative process from idea to expression. Furthermore, each analysis must be taken as such, an analysis as opposed to an interpretation. It is the skeleton or the frame upon with the playwright builds the interpretive resonances (psychological, sociological, etc.) of the dramatic body, intuitively.

The ritual impulses that form the basis of these analyses are as follows:

IDEA-NOTE: what strikes or prompts the playwright's psyche to begin to think in terms of a dramatic expression. This idea-note, amorphous at first, is potent with dramatic possibilities that will become accessible through successive ritual immersions (or forages so to speak) into the *illlud tempus* of the psyche. In a more concrete perception, it is the "kernel" that needs to be cracked to discover its dramatic or ritual contents such as situation, subject, theme, plot, climax, resolution, as well as the psychological, sociological implications that come with them, dependent on the playwright's cultural make-up, social upbringing and experiential influences.

IMAGE: The visual flash that provides a physical or metaphoric specification of the idea-note. It helps the playwright begin to perceive the dramatic potential of the play.

SITUATION: What evolves as an articulation of the incident or incidents within which the playwright could focus his or her dramatic expression. It establishes a possible central character, the ritual circumstance that confronts this person, and the way the character may choose to deal with it.

SUBJECT (of the intended dramatic expression): What the play is about— what is discovered ultimately as the key that strikes the idea-note in the psyche.

THEME (of the intended dramatic expression): What evolves as a concise dramatic definition of the idea-note struck by the subject-key. It is therefore usually expressed with that subject-key.

CENTRAL CHARACTER: An identified individual from the idea-note that promises to define a most important course of action to fulfill a certain need.

OBJECTIVE (of central character): The need central to the most important individual of the expression, and which the individual aspires to achieve through an action, or a series of connected actions he or she executes.

PLOT: The outline of the most important ritual impulse of the idea-note, the physical frame to build and invent interpretive resonances. It maps out for the central character an action or a set of connected actions, subject to challenges, that are crucial to the character's needs and achievement. These actions pose to the playwright and eventually to the audience a major question (the major dramatic question) whether or not the central character will achieve his or her objective.

CLIMAX: The moment in the dramatic explication of the idea-note towards which the objective-action(s) of the central character gravitates. It reveals, to the playwright and ultimately the audience, the possibility or impossibility of the central character achieving his or her objective.

RESOLUTION: The final action open to the playwright and his or her central character, and establishing the character's reaction to the climax.

Note that the ritual impulses and the following analysis of structure are expressed from the point of view of the central character, whose action is the most important in the play. He or she is the doer of the main action of the play. It is this action the playwright tries to ritualize from its roots through its development to its climax, where it becomes apparent whether or not the central character will achieve his or her objective.

1. *Oedipus Rex*

   Idea: Fate concerning a certain quest for truth.

   Image: An egotistic character gorging his eyes out after finding out the truth.

   Situation: A king renown for solving riddles insists on finding out the truth about a present destructive mystery, in spite of the fact the truth critically implicates him. Or,

   –A renown king needs to resolve the mystery of the plague that is destroying his city, even though he may be the cause of the plague.

   Subject: Search for Truth

   Theme: The search for truth, if allowed to intoxicate, may propel a man to destroy himself.

   Central Character: Oedipus

   Central Character's Objective: To find out the truth about the cause of the plague.

   Plot: a. Root Action: Oedipus, informed about the plague that is destroying his city, commits everybody under oath and curse, including himself, to finding out the truth about the cause of the plague.

   b. Developing Action: Oedipus, provoked by the prodding of his heart, which dangerously implicates him, insists on getting to the heart of the mystery.

   (This prodding is caused by Teiresias' pronouncement, and Jocasta's and Messenger from Corinth's revelations)

   —Major Dramatic Question: Will Oedipus know the truth and therefore find relief?

   —Climax (when the MDQ is answered): When Shepherd arrives, truth is inevitable.

   c. Resulting Action: Oedipus gorges out his eyes.

2. *Waiting for Godot*

   Idea (according to Beckett—Saint Augustine's paradoxical palliative): Do not despair, one of the thieves was saved; do not presume, one of the thieves was damned.

   Image: Two tramps waiting for somebody at crossroads.

   Situation: Two tramps waiting for somebody they believe would better their lives do not know whether the person would show up.

   Subject: Waiting or Hoping (for some salvation); Salvation(thematic[2])

   Theme: Waiting or hoping (for salvation) is a chancy endeavor that may or may not produce the expected (technical). Or,

—Salvation has a fifty-fifty chance in achieving (thematic).
Central Character: Estragon and Vladimir (Gogo and Didi).
Central Characters Objective: To wait for Godot for a desired need (technical).
—To hope for salvation (thematic).
Plot: a. Root Action: Gogo and Didi wait in hope for Godot who seems to represent their desired need.
  b. In order to be able to relieve themselves of the boredom of waiting, Gogo and Didi pass the time clowning and capering with themselves, and with passers-by (Pozzo and Lucky).
     —Major Dramatic Question: Will they be able to see Godot and accomplish their needs?
     —Climax: Boy comes the second time to say Godot will not make it that day.
  c. Resulting Action: Gogo and Didi continue to wait.

3. *Zoo Story*
Idea: Suicide through loneliness or isolation—perhaps through an actual report of one such incident in the newspaper.
Image: Various images of loneliness: such as, caged animals in the zoo; lonely man reading a newspaper in Central Park; strained relationship of a lonely man with a dog.
Subject: Loneliness; isolation
Theme: Loneliness (or isolation), through inability to relate with people, can push a person into making a violent statement about his or her condition.
Situation: A lonely man harasses another individual with the view to making a statement about his loneliness, and perchance that of the other individual.
Central Character: Jerry
Central Character's Objective: To make Peter be more aware of loneliness or isolation.
Plot: a. Root Action: Jerry tries to engage Peter's attention in conversation
  b. Developing Action: Having secured Peter's attention, Jerry begins to harass him in various ways.
     —Major Dramatic Question: Will Jerry be able to make Peter aware of loneliness?
     —Climax: When Jerry immolates himself on his knife that Peter is holding. (It is a desperate moment that finally jolts Peter into awareness).
Resulting Action: Jerry commends Peter for finally getting it, and then dies.

4. *A Fool for Love*

Idea: Relationships, hampered with societal constraints, caught between fulfillment and negation

Image: Flashes of love-hate relationship between an insecure young couple because of societal values and taboos; inimical forces (ghosts, collision, explosion) inside and outside of a motel room with a young couple.

Situation: Half-siblings trying to secure a bonding of their love are haunted by the guilt of their innocent but illicit relationship.

Subject: Bonds of Love

Theme: Bonds of love between two people may be difficult to secure because of family or societal constraints.

Central Character: Either Eddie or May

Central Character's Objective:

Eddie: To try and stabilize his relationship with May

May: To try and repel Eddie's advances to stabilize their relationship.

Plot: (If Eddie is the Central Character)
    a. Root Action: Eddie, who has reappeared in May's life after a time lapse, tries to convince May of his intentions to stabilize their relationship.
    b. Developing Action: Eddie, threatened with the possibility of losing May (May taunts him with her expected date and Eddie's affair with a possible Countess; there is an ever-present image of his father which deflates his intentions; May's date actually arrives), desperately tries to override his insecurity with macho tactics even in the face of admission of an incestuous relationship with May.
       —Major Dramatic Question: Will Eddie be able to stabilize his relationship with May?
       —Climax: As Eddie and May embrace and kiss, headlights arc from outside exposing their action; then sound of collision, shattering glass and explosion.
    c. Resulting Action: Eddie leaves.

(If May is the Central Character)
    a. Root Action: May, confronted with the reappearance of Eddie into her life, tries to repel his advances to stabilize their relationship (taunts him with his possible affair with a Countess, and her expectation of a date).
    b. Developing Action: After trying all she could to reject Eddie's claims on her and to get away, May attests to the reality of their incestuous relationship, and concedes to Eddie (in the presence of her date, and despite the looming presence of their discrediting father).

—Major Dramatic Question: Will May be able to repel Eddie
—Climax: Eddie leaves (after the arcing headlights, collision and explosion).
  c. Resulting Action: Confirming Eddie has again disappeared from her life, May leaves with her suitcase.
5. *The America Play*
  Idea: Black people and ironies of history; the Great Hole of History.
  Image: Great Man Lincoln and an African American lookalike. Black persons digging up bones of history.
  Situation: Wife and son digging for historical artifacts of husband/father, an African-American lookalike of Abraham Lincoln who died impersonating the Great Man (technical).
  —A research endeavor that reveals ironic discrepancies of history (thematic).
  Subject: Digging up the past; historical research.
  Theme: Digging up the past of a dead person to resolve mysteries of his life may reveal crucial ironies of greatness and fame (technical)
  —Historical research can be so subjective and full of discrepancies that investigating a greater known person is no more accurate than investigating a lesser known (thematic).
  Central Characters: Lucy and Brazil.
  Central Characters' Objective: To determine certain facts about the Foundling Father, especially relating to his impersonation of Abraham Lincoln.
  Plot: a. Root Action: Lucy and Brazil (at a probable site of Foundling Father's grave) repetitively recall the main enactment of the Foundling Father's impersonation of Abraham Lincoln (with the view to finding out how realistic and worthy is his representation).
    b. Developing Action: As they dig up artifacts of the Foundling Father's impersonation, Lucy and Brazil try to reconstruct the mystery surrounding his person, possible fame and death (with the view to eliciting comparisons between him and the great man of his impersonation).
      —Major Dramatic Question: Will Lucy and Brazil be able to determine the facts they pursue?
      —Climax: They conclude, albeit a conjecture, that the circumstances surrounding the death of Foundling Father are similar to those of Abraham Lincoln[3]
    c. Resulting Action: They inducted the Foundling Father into the Hall of Fame.[4]

As stated, these sets of analysis represent the frame upon which the playwright creatively and intuitively builds what evolves as or becomes interpretive resonances, what enable the reader or the viewer to have different interpretations of a particular playwright's expression. In order to better understand these ritual registers of your creative process, you should try to draw up an analysis of some of your favorite plays, especially those that seem to have made some impact on your creativity.

NOTES

1. The analysis for the most part is based on the one suggested by Bernard Grebanier in book on playwriting. However, for reasons that may be obvious, I have felt the need to modify or extend Professor Grebanier's format, with the hope that my revision further elucidates what Professor Grebanier might have implied but which remained obscure to me. See, Grebanier, *Playwriting: How to Write for the Theater*, ch. 3 and 4.

2. Certain plays, especially ones that focus idea more than action, take on a deliberate metaphoric development in addition or complementary to the normal action-defined structure. I have identified such development as thematic, in contrast to the technical of the action-defined.

3. See *The America Play and Other Works*, 198.

4. See *The America Play*, 199.

Bibliography

BOOKS

Benedetti, Robert. *The Actor at Work*. 4th ed. New York: Prentice-Hall, Inc., 1986.

Brockett, Oscar. *History of Theatre*. 4th ed. Boston, Ma.: Allyn and Bacon, 1982.

Brockett, Oscar. *History of Theatre*. 9th ed. Boston, Ma.: Allyn and Bacon, 1999.

Brokett, Oscar. *The Theatre: An Introduction*. New York: Holt, Rinehart and Winston, Inc., 1969.

Catron, Louis E. *Playwriting: Writing, Producing, and Selling Your Play*. Prospect Heights, Il: Waveland Press, Inc., 1984.

Cohn, Ruby. *Edward Albee*, in *University of Minnesota Pamphlets on American Writers*. Mn.: University of Minnesota Press, 1969.

Cole, David. *The Theatrical Event: A Mythos, A Vocabulary, A Perspective*. Middletown, Ct.: Wesleyan University Press, 1975.

Cole, Toby, and Helen Krich Chinoy, eds. *Directors on Directing*. Revised edition. New York: The Bobbs-Merrill Co., Inc., 1963.

Corrigan, Robert W. *The Theatre in Search of a Fix*. New York: Dell Publishing, 1973.

Eliade, Mircea. *Shamanism: Archaic Techniques of Ecstacy*. Translated by Willard R. Trask. New Jersey: Princeton University Press, 1972.

Esslin, Martin. *Theatre of the Absurd*. New York: Anchor Books, 1969.

Euba, Femi. *Archetypes, Imprecators and Victims of Fate: Origins and Developments of Satire in Black Drama*. Westport, Ct.: Greenwood Press, 1989.

Glenn, Stanley L. *The Complete Actor*. Boston: Allyn and Bacon, Inc., 1977.

Grebanier, Bernard. *Playwriting: How to Write for the Theater*. New York: Harper & Row, 1961.

Lewis, Allan. *American Plays and Playwrights of Contemporary Theatre*. New York: Crown Publishers, 1965.

Frye, Northorpe. *Anatomy of Criticism: Four Essays*. New Jersey: Princeton University Press, 1957.

Habib, Imthiaz. *Shakespeare and Race: Postcolonial Praxis in Early Modern Period.* Lanham, Md.: University Press of America, 2000.

Sainer, Arthur. *The New Radical Theatre Notebook.* New, expanded, revised edition. New York: Applause, 1997.

Shyllon, Folarin O. *Black People in Britain: 1555–1833.* London: Oxford University Press, 1977.

Soyinka, Wole. *Myth, Literature and The African World.* Cambridge, England: Cambridge University Press, 1976.

Tokson, Elliot H. *The Popular Image of the Black Man in English Drama: 1550–1688.* Boston: G.K. Hall, 1982.

Webster's Third New International Dictionary. Unabridged. Springfield, Ma.: Merriam-Webster, Inc., 1986.

ESSAYS

Cowhig, Ruth. "Blacks in English Renaissance and the Role of Shakespeare's *Othello*." *The Black Presence in English Literature*, edited by David Dabydeen. Manchester: Manchester University Press, 1985.

Elliot Butler-Evans. "Haply, for I Am Black": Othello and the Semiotics of Race and Otherness." *Othello: New Essays by Black Writers*, edited by Mythili Kaul. Washington, DC: Howard University Press, 1997.

Ericson, P. "Representation of Blacks and Blackness in the Renaissance." *Criticism*, 35 no. 4 (1992): 499–527.

George, Kathatrine. "The Civilized West Looks at Primitive Africa: 1400–1800." *The Concept of the Primitive*, edited by A Montagu. New York: Free Press, 1968.

Jones, Leroi. "The Revolutionary Theatre." *Home, Social Essays.* New York: William Morrow, 1966.

Kermode, Frank."Othello, the Moor of Venice." 1198–1202 in *The Riverside Shakespeare*, edited by G. Blakemore Evans, et al. Boston: Houghton Mifflin, 1974.

Neal, Larry. "The Black Arts Movement." *The Drama Review* 12, no. 4 (Summer 1968): 29–39.

Nelson, Hugh. "Leroi Jones' *Dutchman*: A Brief Ride on a Doomed Ship." *Educational Journal* 20, no. 1 (March, 1968): 53–59.

Soyinka, Wole. "Introduction." *The Bacchae of Euripides: A Communion Rite.* New York: W.W. Norton, 1974.

PLAYS

Aeschylus. *The Orestes Plays of Aeschylus*, translated by Paul Roche. New York: Penguin-Mentor 1962.

Albee, Edward. *The Zoo Story and the Sandbox.* New York: Dramatists Play Service, 1960.

Beckett, Samuel. *Waiting for Godot*. New York: Grove Press, 1982.
Evans, G. Blakemore, ed. *The Riverside Shakespeare*. Boston: Houghton Mifflin, 1974.
Finlay, Fiona, ed. *Single Voices*: *The Book of the TV Series*. London: BBC Books, 1990.
Grene, David and Richmond Lattimore, eds. *Sophocles I*. 2nd ed. Chicago: The University of Chicago Press, 1991.
Jones, Leroi (Amiri Baraka). *Dutchman and The Slave*. New York: Morrow/Quill, 1964.
Parks, Suzan-Lori. *The America Play and Other Works*. New York: Theatre Communications Group, Inc., 1995.
Pirandello, Luigi. *Pirandello's Major Plays*. Evanston, Il: Northwestern University Press, 1991.
Sartre, Jean-Paul. *No Exit and Other Plays*. New York: Vintage International, 1989.
Shakespeare, William. *As You Like It*, edited by Agnes Latham. London: Methuen & Co., 1975.
——. *Hamlet, Prince of Denmark*. Cambridge: Cambridge University Press, 1985.
——. *King Lear*, edited by Kenneth Muir. London: Methuen, 1972.
——. *Othello*, edited by M. R. Ridley. London: Methuen, 1958.
——. *Twelfth Night*, edited by George L. Kittredge. 2nd ed. Waltham, Ma.: Blaisdell Publishing Co., 1966.
——. *The Tempest*, edited by Stephen Orgel. Oxford: Clarendon Press, 1987.
Shepard, Sam. *Fool for Love and Other Plays*. New York: Bantam Books, 1984.
Soyinka, Wole. *The Bacchae of Euripides*: *A Communion Rite*. New York: W.W. Norton, 1974.
Williams, Tennessee. *The Glass Menagerie*. New York: Dramatist Publishing, 1975.

Index

Aaron (*Titus Andronicus*), 39
abstractions, 6–11, 16, 20–22, 28, 53–54, 66–67, 69, 74, 132
absurdist vision, 43–44, 46, 47, 64, 82
action, 11, 37–38, 63, 69, 75–79, 84, 150–51. *See also* objective-action
The Actor at Work (Benedetti), 79
actors, 7–8, 14–15, 28–29, 48, 49, 96–97, 127, 130
The Adding Machine (Rice), 17
Adler, Richard, 17
Aeschylus, 89, 99
African characters, 92
Albee, Edward, 42–44, 108, 117, 118. *See also The Zoo Story* (Albee)
The America Play (Parks), 46, 68–72, 82–86, 154–55
Antigone (Sophocles), 35
Apollo, 60, 81
Ariel, 25–29, 38–39
Aristotle, 7
art forms, 4–5
assimilation, 44–45
As You Like It (Shakespeare), 98
audiences: acceptance of, 41, 49, 100–102, 105, 114, 118, 126–27, 130; playwright's responsibility to, 74; and plot structure of *Waiting for Godot*, 65; responses of, 55–56, 89–91, 93–96, 109
autobiography, 43, 55

The Bacchae of Euripides (Soyinka), 99
Beckett, Samuel, 8, 11, 37–38, 63–69, 82, 84, 85. *See also Waiting for Godot* (Beckett)
Benedetti, Robert, 79
Brabantio, 120, 121
Brazil (*The America Play*), 69–71, 83–85, 154
Brook, Peter, 6, 17

Caliban (*The Tempest*), 39
catharsis, 48–49
characters: actions of, 150–51; in *The America Play*, 69–71, 84; black, 39–46, 68–69, 92; and climax of plot, 62–63; communication of playwright's objective, 74–79, 85, 127; communication of theme, 64–65; definition of central, 150; development of, 118, 132–34, 140; dialogue between, 111–13; expression of impulses through, 52, 55–62; fate of, 31, 33–36, 47–48; interpretation of *illud tempus*, 15, 49,

110; location of, 97–101; in one-act plays, 108–11, 114, 122; and playwright's attitude toward idea-note, 28–29; and ritual implements, 122–28
The Chemist (Clarke), 95, 98, 102–3, 105–8
chorus dancers, 18
Cinthio, Giraldi, 39–41
clarity, 130
Clarke, Roy, 95, 105–8. *See also The Chemist* (Clarke)
climax, 62–63, 150
Cole, David, 5, 7–8, 15, 29
comedy, 17, 94
complications, 122–23
conflict, 79, 80
Corrigan, Robert W., 9, 36
Creon, 35, 81

Day of Absence (Ward), 46
deadline, 79, 80
Death of a Salesman (Miller), 106
descriptive form, 21
Desdemona, 39–40, 120
dialogue, 111–13, 126–27
Didi, 36–38, 64–68, 97, 126, 152
Dionysus, 9–10, 18
directors, 7–8, 14–15, 28, 49, 77, 100, 127, 130
dithyramb, 18
drama: definition of, 3; fundamental elements of, 79–87; as myth, 32–33; relationship to other art forms, 4–5
Dutchman (Jones), 42–45
Duxley, Vernon, 95, 98, 102–3, 105–8

Eddie (*A Fool for Love*), 46–47, 108–11, 114–16, 118–19, 125, 153–54
efficacy, 23–30
"elation of success," 10
Eliade, Mircea, 15
emotion, 123–24, 126–27
European dramatic tradition, 5–6, 19
experiences, 55–56

factual perception, 43, 47
fateful/fatal paradox, 31–51; absurdity of, 64; in creative process, 8–12, 47–48; in *A Fool for Love*, 46–47; need to investigate, 20; in *Oedipus Rex*, 10, 34–36, 56–62, 99; in *Othello*, 38–42, 60; and ritual, 18, 19, 53–54; in *Waiting for Godot*, 10–11, 36–38; in *Zoo Story* and *Dutchman*, 43–45
The Flies (Sartre), 99
A Fool for Love (Shepard), 46–47, 108–11, 114–19, 153
Foundling Father, 69–72, 83, 154
Frye, Northorp, 5, 32
full-length plays, 104, 108, 115–25, 139–40

gestures, 127–28
Girod, Kelley, 141
The Glass Menagerie (Williams), 107
Gogo, 36–38, 64–68, 126, 152
Grebanier, Bernard, 95
Greek theater, 99–100

Hamlet (Shakespeare), 88, 91, 118
Hansberry, Lorraine, 46
"happy idea," 59–60, 114
history, 68–72, 83–85

Iago, 40, 41, 42, 60, 121
idea-based drama, 11
idea-dramatic, 63
idealism, 46–47
idea-narrative, 70
idea-note: for *The America Play*, 69; and audiences of monologues, 91; of black playwrights, 44–46; and complications, 122–23; in creative process, 10–11; definition of, 3–4, 149; and development of full-length plays, 119–20; and dramatic structure, 52; expression of, 31–32, 47–49, 54–58, 105; and gestures, 127; interpretation of, 14–19; of

LeRoi Jones, 42–45; and need, 20–22; and objective, 78–79; for *Oedipus Rex*, 35; in one-character plays, 90, 91; for *Othello*, 39–40, 120, 122; playwright's attitude toward, 27–29; and textual analysis, 149; and theme, 134–35; and visible constructs, 12; for *Waiting for Godot*, 36–38; for *Zoo Story*, 42–44

illud tempus: components of, 11, 15; definition of, 8, 9; exercises relating to, 131–32; interpretation of, 14–15, 19, 48–49; and music, 18; revisions of, 129–30; and ritual process, 15–17; and script, 28–29; and theme, 134; through characters, 15, 49, 110

images, 27, 35, 47, 60, 67–69, 132, 150
imagination, 21, 24
incidents, 115–17, 121–22
individuality, 21
inspiration, 4, 6, 13
interpretation, 7–8, 14–17, 19, 23–24
isolation, 43–44, 111–13, 116–19, 125

Jerry (*Zoo Story*), 44, 111–13, 116–19, 125, 152
Jocasta, 60, 62
Joe Turner's Come and Gone (Wilson), 46
Jones, LeRoi, 42–45

language. *See* voice
Lincoln, Abraham, 69–72, 83, 154
Liquid Theater, 17
location, 97–101
love, 5, 12, 21, 40, 46–47, 119
Lucky, 11, 65–67
Lucy (*The America Play*), 69–71, 83–85, 154

Macbeth (Shakespeare), 113
Mahabarata (Brook), 17
Major Dramatic Question (MDQ), 62
Marlene (*The Chemist*), 107–8

May (*A Fool for Love*), 46–47, 108–11, 114–16, 125, 153–54
The Merchant of Venice (Shakespeare), 76
metaphysical. *See* abstractions
monologues: audiences of, 93–96, 109; challenges of, 103; characteristics of, 88–90; development of, 106–8, 113; exercises for, 90–92, 104, 138–39, 141–47; location of, 97–101; monotonic, 24–27, 75, 91–93, 96, 104, 135–38; objective-action in, 105–8; and present time, 101–3; voice of, 96–97, 126–27
Mourning Becomes Electra (O'Neill), 99
music, 5–6, 17–18, 24–30, 68–69
myth: in drama, 32–36; and expression of impulses, 56–58; in *Oedipus Rex*, 61–63; in *Othello*, 39–42; and perception, 43, 47; in *Waiting for Godot*, 37–38; in *Zoo Story* and *Dutchman*, 43–45
Myth, Literature and the African World (Soyinka), 5

narrative form, 21, 32–33
need, 20–22
No Exit (Sartre), 33

objective, 74–81, 85, 90, 109–13, 150
objective-action: in *The America Play*, 83–85; connection with audience through, 130; and emotion, 124; expression of ritual impulses through, 56–58; in monologues, 113; in *Oedipus Rex*, 61–63; in one-act plays, 105–8, 117–19; in *Othello*, 121; stylistic approaches to, 85, 86; in *Waiting for Godot*, 65, 82. *See also* action
Oedipus Rex (Sophocles): characters in, 118, 124–25; dramatic elements in, 80–82, 84, 85; emotion in, 124; expression of playwright's

experiences and impulses in, 56–61; fateful/fatal paradox in, 10, 34–36, 56–62, 99; location of, 99–100; plot structure of, 61–63; as subject of study, 8–9; textual analysis of, 151

Ogun, 9–10, 53, 74–75

one-act monologues, 12, 89, 93, 95, 96, 102–4, 106–8, 138–39, 141–47

one-act plays: creation from full-length plays, 120–22; language in, 126–27; objective-action in, 105–8, 117–19; situations in, 115–17

one-character plays, 89–90, 93, 96, 103. *See also* monologues

O'Neill, Eugene, 99

Opera Theater, 17

opposites, 21

Othello (Shakespeare), 38–42, 60, 81–82, 85, 99–100, 120–22, 124, 125

The Pajama Game (Adler and Ross), 17

Parks, Suzan-Lori, 46, 68–72, 82–86. *See also The America Play* (Parks)

personal stakes, 79, 80

Peter (*Zoo Story*), 44, 111–13, 116, 152

Pirandello, Luigi, 33

playwrights: black, 44–46, 68–69, 85; complications of, 122–23; marginalization of, 2–4; objectivity of, 23; revisions by, 129–30

plot, 52, 61–69, 102, 149, 150

Pozzo, 11, 37, 65–68

Prospero, 24–25, 28, 38–39, 118

A Raisin in the Sun (Hansberry), 46

realism, 48–49, 91, 96–97

reality, 32–33, 38, 43, 47

re-creation, 20, 24, 32

religion, 63–64, 67

repetition and revision, 69–70, 85

resolution, 150

"The Revolutionary Theatre" (Jones), 45

Rice, Elmer, 17

ritual implements, 122–28

ritual impulses, 4; expression of playwright's, 55–60, 72; and plot structure, 61–63; and textual analysis, 149–51; and transformation of idea-note, 52; in *Waiting for Godot*, 63–68

ritual process, 19–30; in determining objective, 78–79; efficacy in, 23–30; and expression of idea-note, 31–32, 47–49, 53, 105; and fateful/fatal paradox, 18, 19, 53–54; and *illud tempus*, 15–17; and imposed point of view, 33–34; influences on, 1–13; monologue development through, 113; need in, 20–22; in one-character plays, 90; and playwright's skills, 41–42; power of, 17–18; and revisions, 129; and textual analysis, 149; in *Zoo Story*, 44

ritual scope, 115–25, 139–40

Romeo and Juliet (Shakespeare), 12

Ross, Jerry, 17

sacrifice, 22, 25–27, 48

Saint Augustine, 37, 38, 63–65

Sartre, Jean Paul, 33, 99

Schectner, Richard, 6

script, 15, 18, 28–29, 129–30

Shakespeare, William: complexity of, 115; gestures in plays of, 127; and location, 98–100; on music, 5, 24–29; questions of central character in *Merchant of Venice*, 76; use of dramatic elements, 80–82, 85; use of fateful/fatal complex, 38–42, 60; use of monologue, 113

Shepard, Sam, 46–47, 108–11, 114, 116, 118. *See also A Fool for Love* (Shepard)

situation, 115–17, 120–21, 133–34, 150

Six Characters in Search of an Author (Pirandello), 33

The Slave (Jones), 45–46

Sophocles, 8–9, 34–36, 56–63, 80–82, 84, 85, 89, 99–100. *See also Oedipus Rex* (Sophocles)
Soyinka, Wole, 5–6, 9, 17–18, 24, 49, 53, 74, 99
spirituality, 7, 18–21, 24, 54
spontaneity, 4
structure. *See* plot
stylistic approaches, 85–86
subject, 58–59, 120, 134–35, 150
subjective/accommodating response, 56
surreal vision, 44–45

technology, 16–17
Teiresias, 60, 62, 81
The Tempest (Shakespeare), 24–29, 38–39, 118
textual analysis, 149–55
theme, 58–59, 64–72, 86, 119–20, 130, 134–35, 150
Thespis, 24, 89
time, present, 101–3, 113–14
Titus Andronicus (Shakespeare), 39

tragedy, 9, 17, 35–40, 42
Turner, Victor, 6
Twelfth Night (Shakespeare), 5

urgency, 79, 80

visible constructs, 11–12, 119–20
voice, 24, 54, 90–93, 96–97, 126–27. *See also* dialogue; monologues

Waiting for Godot (Beckett), 8, 10–11, 36–38, 63–69, 82, 84, 85, 97, 125–26, 151–52
Ward, Douglas Turner, 46
Wessels, Walker, 45
Who's Afraid of Virginia Woolf, 117
will, dramatic, 74–76, 78
Williams, Tennessee, 107
Wilson, August, 46

Yoruba, 5, 9, 18–19, 24, 53

The Zoo Story (Albee), 42–45, 108, 111–19, 125, 152–53